On the Threshold of Grace

Methodist Fundamentals

Donald W. Haynes

"When first sent forth to minister the word,
Say, did we preach ourselves, or Christ the Lord?
Was it our aim disciples to collect
To raise a party, or to found a sect?
No, but to spread the power of Jesus' name,
Repair the walls of our Jerusalem
Revive the piety of ancient days,
And fill the earth with our Redeemer's praise."

— Charles Wesley, 1743

Published by UMR Communications

1221 Profit Drive

Dallas, TX 75247 U.S.A.

ISBN: 978-0-9845499-0-0

TABLE OF CONTENTS

In Memoriam

Treva Joy Williams Haynes
1897-1989

Winnie Mae Lawing Parker
1906-1998

Joan's and my mothers who rocked us

In Methodist cradles

Nurtured us in John Wesley

And led us to Christ

INTRODUCTION

"By rule they eat, by rule they drink,
Do all things else by rule, but think—
…Method alone must guide 'em all,
Whence Methodists themselves they call."[1]

In this booklet of Methodist fundamentals, we use the term "Methodist" generically rather than to identify a specific denomination. We hope it will be helpful for all who bear the word Methodist in their denominations as well as for Wesley's children who do not use the term Methodist in their names — Nazarenes, Wesleyans, former Evangelical United Brethren, Assemblies of God, etc. All are Arminian, not Calvinists. All embrace what we call "grace theology." The title that John Wesley would give these fundamentals would be "Scriptural Way of Salvation." We are attempting here to recover Wesleyan heritage.

We also hope the book will be helpful to seekers — to those searching for the meaning of life, searching the Scriptures for their own way of salvation — and for every pilgrim who needs some guide in how these "people called Methodists" found what Charles Wesley called "love divine, all loves excelling, joy of heaven to earth come down." This is the Wesleyan way to a "purpose-driven life," grounded in God's indefatigable love, but one need not be a Methodist to find them helpful.

United Methodist Bishop Kenneth Carder has observed that 80 percent of questions coming to his desk "focused on theology, beliefs and doctrines; very few questions were about structures, apportionments, or the pastoral appointment process."[2] Wesley himself feared in his last years "not that Methodism would cease to exist but it might become "a dead sect with the form of religion but without its power."

My seminary students reflect a sad ignorance of Methodist fundamentals. At the same time, I wince when I hear my own grandchildren echo the influences of fundamentalism on their spiritual journey. These are some of the influential voices that moved me as a septuagenarian to write.

Who is a Methodist?

In the 1830s, Scottish Presbyterian Thomas Chalmers wrote, "Methodism is Christianity in earnest."[3] We hardly deserve that compliment today, but Chalmers' comment piques my interest. What in our rich heritage would bring that accolade from a man of Chalmers' stature? His words raise the question anew: "What are the fundamentals of Methodism?"

Wesley himself asked when he laid the cornerstone of Wesley Chapel in London:

> What is Methodism? Is it not a new religion? Nothing could be further from the truth. Methodism… is the old religion, the religion of the Bible, the religion of the primitive Church… none other than the love of God and of all mankind.[4]

In response to the rising tide of fundamentalism in the 1920s, Bishop Edwin Mouzon struck the proper balance: "It is one thing to be charitable in reference to theological opinions, and it is another and a different thing to be lax."[5] He added:

> Methodism lays down no theological requirement for Church membership and allows large liberty of thinking. But belief in the essential facts of Christianity is, of course, necessary to being a Christian. United Methodism rests on a solid foundation of Apostolic, Protestant, and Wesleyan fundamentals of belief, experience, and practice.[6]

When the three branches of Methodism united in 1939, Edwin Lewis of Drew University spoke wisely when he said, "There is always the danger that the fascination of the new will lead to less than justice being done to the well-tried old."[7] He added, "It is our right, perhaps our obligation to look at the whole long history… but if at the same time we also reject the faith that inspired that history, we cannot escape the charge that we have broken at a vital point with the testimony of Christian tradition."[8]

Gilbert Rowe of Duke Divinity School gave us a timeless definition of Methodism:

> It is the most persistent and successful attempt that has ever been made to separate between the essential and the nonessential, to concentrate upon the essence of the Christian religion. …Having learned that salvation is the possession of the Spirit of Jesus through experience, Methodism intends to allow nothing to interfere with or obscure this truth. The culminating doctrine of Methodism is the witness of the Spirit.[9]

The world is waiting for a church that can market that message! We have an opportunity to seize the moment for major personal and cultural impact. American culture today offers Methodism an unprecedented opportunity for what our ancestors called "holy boldness." In *The Faith We Declare*, Lewis wrote, "'In Christ' is the relationship by whose light we read God, and in whose light we will read ourselves."[10] Seventy years later, this remains a Methodist fundamental.

Former Duke Divinity School Dean Robert Cushman insisted that the distinguishing marks of a Methodist are not "opinions," even true ones, but by "experiencing God's saving grace in Christ, as it is revealed by the inner workings of the Holy Spirit." He quotes from Wesley's letter to Conyers Middleton:

'To believe (in the Christian sense) is, then, to... have a clear sight of God, and confidence in the most High, reconciled to me through the Son of his Love.' Accordingly, it is manifest to the Wesleys that saving faith is the effectual work of the Holy Spirit and... the believer has a sure confidence that his sins are forgiven and he is reconciled. Wesley had not known this himself until 1738, but he then found it to be 'the fundamental doctrine' of the Church, the 'scriptural way of salvation,' and, along with sanctification, the core doctrine of 'experimental and practical divinity.'[11]

"If there were no sin," Cushman added, "there would be no relevance of this gospel, but since sin is rampant in every generation, the Methodists believe that the truth of this gospel is best expressed as 'taking the cure.'"[12] We believe that "living faith" is superior to simply a faith that is believed. To his former devotion to Scripture, tradition and reason, Wesley experienced grace at Aldersgate. He called the Methodist expression of salvation "practical divinity."

Cushman closes the last book he ever wrote with ominous words, "The spectacular decline of membership in The United Methodist Church during the past decade and more may suggest that very many are wearied beyond endurance with a church that manages mainly 'the form of godliness,' on the one hand and seems doctrinally shapeless on the other."[13] Russell Richey, a pre-eminent historian of American United Methodism, says that the emphasis of Methodism in the 19th century was missions and evangelism, and in the 20th century was ecumenism. I believe the hour has come, in the words of Isaac, to "redig the wells of our fathers."

Ted Campbell, Perkins School of Theology professor of church history, is only one of a new breed of scholars who are taking us back to John Wesley. He writes, "In describing his vision of a 'catholic spirit' John Wesley distinguished between *essential* doctrines and *opinions* about theology or church practices."[14] Campbell cites Wesley's insistence on the Trinity, human need for grace, the sacraments, and "doctrines that define the particular spirituality and teachings of the Methodist movement (especially those teachings of the 'way of salvation' including preparing, justifying, and sanctifying grace.")[15]

The message of United Methodism has been blurred. We retained our frontier methodology, but let our message erode. William Abraham, a son of Irish Methodism who now teaches at Perkins, laments Methodism's "doctrinal amnesia." Author Diana Butler Bass compares her home United Methodist Church with "the Rotary Club at prayer." She says, "Few United Methodists can provide a conversational synopsis of 'who' the UMC is!" We want to provide such a conversational synopsis!

Wesley's "Scriptural Way of Salvation"

As John Wesley gave shape and content to Methodism's understanding of the "scriptural way of salvation," he preached and taught a different journey for new Christians than he had experienced himself. From his university years through Aldersgate (1725-38), Wesley followed Jesus through personal and social holiness as a disciplined life. His post-Aldersgate preaching and tract-writing reversed that chronology. In the shaping of Methodism, his "order of salvation" was first to accept God's love through an awakening of the soul, then repent; then move through a growing relationship with the Lord. We will elaborate further on the following, but here is a synopsis of Wesley's "scriptural way of salvation."

First, the foundation of our salvation is in the **character of God**. God is sovereign and chooses to express his sovereignty through love, with freedom as his gift. Wesley cited Genesis 1:27 for his affirmation that we are made in God's own image, which includes "human liberty" and what we often call "free will."

Secondly, Wesley and all Methodists insist that God's love is a "seeking love." We see this in the three parables of Luke 15: the lost coin, the lost sheep, the lost boy. Human liberty and God's seeking love are dimensions of what we call **"prevenient"** or **preparing grace.**

Thirdly, if we respond to the convicting call of the Holy Spirit we can repent and *know* our sins forgiven. This is **"saving"** or **justifying grace**. We see this in many Scriptures, one being I John: "If we confess our sins, he is faithful and just to forgive us our sins and cleanse us from all unrighteousness."

Fourthly, we begin the disciplined "holiness of life and heart," which, for Wesley, had come first. Paul uses the metaphor of "putting on the whole armor of God." In our grace theology, we call this **"perfecting" grace.**

Fifthly, Jesus moved the goal post to the ultimate: "Be perfect as your father in heaven is perfect" (Matthew 5:48). We seek the high calling that is ours in Christ, to have the mind in us that was in Christ Jesus **— perfect love**.

Wesley summarized his theology as "grace upon grace." He used the metaphor of "porch" for **prevenient** grace, threshold for **saving** grace, and every room of the house for **perfecting** grace. By this metaphor he meant that God seeks that God's will be done in every dimension of our life. To attain this, Wesley outlined what he called "means of grace."

Methodist Fundamentals

In his posthumously published book, *Experimental Divinity,* Robert Cushman insisted that early Methodism was clear about its doctrine. He called this consensus of faith *"consensus fidelium."*[16] We hope in this booklet to recover that *consensus fidelium*, that dual spiritual journey of faith and faithfulness. We believe that combination to be the true identity of the people called Methodists and the genius of all branches of Methodism. Let us now explore the fundamentals of

Methodist doctrine.

The marketing world talks about the necessity of "branding." This is just as important for churches as it is for colleges and universities, for Lexus and Starbucks! To many inside and outside United Methodism, our image is "vanilla." Our strength has become our weakness. Because we have such a large umbrella, our theological trumpet plays an uncertain sound.

Methodism could be what Butler Bass calls, "Christianity for the rest of us." We cannot define Methodist holiness by a straitjacket of moralism or legalism — such as dress codes and a withdrawal from the public square of the religious marketplace. This does not mean, however, that we are a theological sieve or that we must remain mute about our beliefs. We often refer to Wesley's "catholic spirit" as evidence that Methodists can believe just anything. That is not true. What Wesley called "the catholic spirit" is important: "If thy heart is as mine, give me thy hand." Wesley insisted, as we still must, "Though we may not think alike, can we not love alike?"

Yet Wesley warned against being "driven to and fro and tossed about with every wind of doctrine." He was clear:

> You who call yourselves of 'catholic spirit' only because you are of a muddy understanding, because your mind is all in a mist, because you have no settled, consistent principles, be convinced that you have missed the way; you know not where you are. You think you are into the Spirit of Christ when in truth, you are nearer the spirit of Antichrist. Go first and learn the basic elements of the gospel of Christ; and then shall you learn to be of a truly catholic spirit.[17]

Wesley scholar and theologian Albert Outler of Perkins School of Theology distilled this for us with his insistence that Methodism has "a marrow of doctrine" that is distinctively Wesleyan and Arminian. Having said that, Methodism proudly remembers Wesley's insistence that orthodoxy alone is not "true religion." In his sermon "The Way to the Kingdom," Methodism's founder preached:

> Neither does religion consist in orthodoxy or right opinions;
> which are not in the heart but the understanding. A man may
> be orthodox at every point; he may not only espouse right
> opinions, but zealously defend them; he may think justly
> concerning the Incarnation of our Lord, the ever-blessed
> Trinity, and every other doctrine contained in holy writ… and
> yet it is possible he may have no religion at all… and may
> all the while be as great a stranger as the devil himself to the
> religion of the heart.[18]

Summarizing that sermon, Wesley said "true religion" was that point
at which:

> God hath spoken to thy heart, 'Be of good cheer, thy sins are
> forgiven. Thou hast righteousness and peace and joy in the
> Holy Ghost…. Then the love of God is shed abroad in thy
> heart. Thou lovest him because he first loved us. And because
> thou lovest God, thou lovest thy brother also. Indeed thou art
> changed into that glorious image wherein thou wast created.[19]

Though Wesley's words use the medium of Shakespearean English,
their message expresses the essence of Methodism. The bottom line:
Methodism has a doctrine, but we believe that true religion is not
limited either to rational conclusions of the head or the enthusiasm of
the heart. We believe in a marriage of the cognitive and the emotive,
the head and the heart. Between churches centered in sacramentalism
and churches centered in enthusiasm, Methodism is a "middle way."

Millions today feel that life has lost its meaning, its purpose, its
core beliefs. In a culture with more stress yet less meaning, people
yearn for the anchor of certainties. When we are adrift at sea, we will
grab any piece of flotsam for a lifesaver. Any preacher, author, or
denomination that provides this guarantee of religious absolutism
will undoubtedly make converts in a world awash with relativism.
But in response to fundamentalism, we cannot cast stones or assume

an ostrich posture. Rather, Methodism must renew its "experimental divinity," match it with visionary confidence, and revive its mission — to follow Jesus, make disciples, and transform the world.

The time has come for all Methodists to do our homework, to stand up and to speak out! We must lose our timidity, get our message straight and share it — politely, respectfully, but with conviction. We must practice a radical hospitality that includes personal follow-up of worship guests and interpersonal faith sharing. We must preach the Good News!

Jesus met each person where they were; he did not have a "cookie-cutter" message or approach. Our evangelism begins in relationship and must remain there. However, in the context of a caring relationship, there is a core message to convey. We can define our brand in the marketplace of religious theologies and our doctrinal fundamentals without becoming fundamentalists. We can know who we are, claim that, teach that, and find the meaning of life in the context of God's saving grace.

Perhaps one place to look for our fundamentals is the Restrictive Rules (¶'s 17-22 *Book of Discipline*). In defining Methodist fundamentals, the Restrictive Rules forbid future General Conferences to "establish any new standards or rules of doctrine contrary to our present existing and established standards of doctrine." That rule has been somewhat eased down a slippery slope, but Cushman called it the *consensus fidelium* of the Methodist Episcopal Church in 1808!

Cushman says this consensus "embodies the 'sufficient reason' for the church's being" and warns that "the dimming, or decline, or erosion of that consensus is a negative prognosis for the survival of that church, particularly in modern secular society." He questions whether in the absence of this *consensus fidelium,* any "Christian community can attain or retain a manifest identity and self-understanding, or convey a recognizable or enduring message, or, indeed to survive at all."[20]

The United Methodist Church's new "Rethink Church" advertising campaign challenges us to seek common ground within the denomination. Since the days of Outler, more than a hundred volumes have been published that point us again toward Wesley. Though "proof texts" from his sermons, notes, letters, and diaries may lead us to different conclusions, we are still identified by what Wesley called an "experimental divinity."

Part of the United Methodist identity is the inseparability of doctrines and personal discipline. Saying "Jesus has forgiven me of my sins" is just the first step in the way of salvation. Being saved must be followed by growth in grace, which expresses itself in the ethics of Matthew 25 and the discipline of Ephesians 6. Wesley insisted on doing no harm, avoiding evil of every kind, doing good of every possible sort, and attending all the ordinances of the Church. Through Bishop Reuben Job and others, we are recovering this imperative to "walk the walk." As Randy Maddox, professor of theology and Methodist studies at Duke Divinity School, reminds us, "Wesley insisted on a dynamic interrelationship between God's justifying grace and our co-operant response."[21] Wesley connected "saving doctrine" with "living faith" as cooperant dimensions of the "scriptural way of salvation."

Wesley clearly insisted that Methodists maintain active participation in what he called the "ordinary means of grace": Communion, prayer, searching the Scriptures and "attendance upon the public worship of God." But as Maddox insists, "the mature Wesley integrated sacramentalist and evangelical emphases."

Interestingly, Outler's famed "quadrilateral" is not a Methodist fundamental. It is neither doctrinal nor Wesleyan, because it lacks specificity of content. Abraham argues that it is "precarious in the extreme to argue that it is constitutive of Wesley's theology."[22] It is simply a vehicle for checking one's doctrine. For Wesley, all doctrine must be "saving doctrine" and all faith must be "living faith," both of which were dimensions of a renovated life. Outler himself never intended the quadrilateral to be the "sum and summary" of our Methodist fundamentals.

Note to Readers

As you finish each chapter, ask yourself a few questions:

1. What was said that might have prompted you to respond, "Hmm. I never thought of that before"?

2. What bothered you most in this chapter?

3. What was the most helpful or encouraging word for you in this chapter?

4. Upon reading this and reflecting on Wesley and the Scripture passages cited, did you find your concept of God changing?

5. What quote did you highlight?

6. What in the chapter motivated you to get into the Word and dig out more scriptural meanings?

"My remnant of days I spend to His praise
Who died the whole world to redeem;
Be they many or few,
My days are His due,
And they all are devoted to Him!"

Wesley at 84
June 28, 1788

"I am a brand, plucked from the burning."

CHAPTER 1:
Methodism Begins With John Wesley

"I felt my heart strangely warmed. I felt I did trust in Christ, Christ alone for salvation and an assurance was given me that he had taken away my sins, even mine, and saved me from the law of sin and death."
— John Wesley, May 24, 1738

The message and mission of Methodism began with a man, John Wesley (1703-1791). We cannot define Methodism's fundamentals without reference to Wesley and his own spiritual journey. The foundation of Methodist doctrine is the Articles of Religion that Wesley abridged from the Anglican Church. Thus our doctrine is rooted in a "middle way" between the Catholic Church's teachings about spiritual discipline and the Protestant Reformation's insistence on "justification by faith."

John Wesley was spiritually nurtured in a devout, learned, and rather rigidly disciplined Anglican family. His mother was as learned and well read as his Oxford-educated father. Both were very stern — not much affection was expressed in the Wesley family!

The first "rise" of Methodism was at Oxford University — an academic setting that has remained influential in each generation of Methodist development.[1] Wesley called for uniting "those two so long kept separate, knowledge and vital piety."

The term "Methodist" came from the derisive catcalls of Oxford University students who mocked the "holy living" of a campus group who were sometimes called "Bible Moths," "the Enthusiasts," and the "Godly Club." This evolved into the derisive term "Holy Club," which John Wesley himself never used — he detested the word "club" for an inclusive campus group. But the name that stuck from doggerel was "Methodists." Halford Luccock, a

Congregationalist, wrote of the Oxford Methodists:

> Colleges tend to turn out machine-made goods — graduates
> who dress alike, think alike, talk alike, act alike, and all on
> a dead-level of mediocrity. But every so often, there come
> men and women who refuse to wear the clothes, physical or
> mental, that are the mode of the moment. They lead a lonely
> life, but, as on the Lincoln College quad, future students and
> tourists will point to the bust under the windowsill of an
> ordinary dorm room and say, 'That is where the Holy Club
> met.'[2]

With his baccalaureate degree from Christ College, John Wesley
became a deacon and priest in the Church of England, an ordination
he retained until his death. Then he was made a "fellow" at Lincoln
College, Oxford. In 1736, General Oglethorpe appointed him
chaplain of the ship that would take him to his new appointment —
Christ Church in Savannah, Georgia.

The second "rise" of Methodism was Wesley's twenty-two months
of missionary ministry in Georgia (Feb. 6, 1736-Christmas Eve,
1737). On board ship en route, he was deeply impressed by the quiet
resolve of the fifty-nine German Moravians during a storm at sea.
As parish priest, he continued his insistence that Christianity is a
disciplined life of personal holiness accompanied by acts of Christian
mercy, which he called "social holiness."[3] Wesley would weave into
Methodism this Anglo-Catholic spiritual journey, which he always
called "holiness of heart and life." During this time he searched the
Scriptures, baptized babies by trine immersion, asked for confession
before Communion if you had been absent a while, fasted, and met
with the Moravians.

Back in London, in the dead of winter in 1738, he felt himself a failure
and sought the spiritual counsel of Moravian Peter Bohler. Wesley's
cognitive belief in Jesus as his Savior and his spiritual discipline were
in place, but doctrine and discipline alone were less than satisfying.

Wesley needed the confidence that God loved him. His troubled soul sought inner peace, and his anguish was in his lack of that "blessed assurance" that his sins were forgiven.

The third "rise" of Methodism was May 24, 1738, in that Moravian small group Bible study and prayer meeting on Aldersgate Street. After years of spiritual journeying, Wesley finally reported that at "about a quarter to nine, I felt my heart strangely warmed." The watchword of Methodism became that experience of God's grace wherein we "know" our sins forgiven. Aldersgate was followed by Wesley's outdoor preaching and the beginning of "the people called Methodists."

Methodism has often ventured from what Wesley called the "scriptural way of salvation." But whenever we have recovered our voice, enjoyed the quiet confidence of saving grace, and folded assurance into discipleship, Methodism has had a vital message, seen lives changed dramatically, and greatly influenced societal culture. Therefore, we must look anew at who we are, what we believe, and how — in the words of William Sangster of London — "Methodism can be born again."[4]

"I abhor the doctrine of predestination, a doctrine upon the supposition of which, if one could possibly suppose it for a moment (call it election, reprobation, or whatever you please, for all comes to the same thing). No scripture can mean that God is not love, or that his mercy is not over all his works. That is, whatever, it prove beside, no Scripture can prove predestination."

"**...the soul that chooseth life shall live, as the soul that chooseth death shall die.** This decree yields the strongest encouragement to abound in all good works, and in all holiness, and it is a wellspring of joy, of happiness also, to our great and endless comfort. This is worthy of God. It is every way consistent with all the perfections of God's nature. It gives us the noblest view of his justice, mercy, and truth. To this agrees the whole scope of the Christian revelation.

"For if a sick man knows that he must unavoidable die or unavoidably recover, ...it is not reasonable for him to take any physic [medicine] at all. He might justly say, 'If I am ordained to life, I shall live; if to death, I shall die. So I need not trouble myself about it.'"

Thus our blessed Lord: "If any man thirst, let him come to me and drink." (John 7:37).
Thus his great Apostle, Paul: "God commandeth **all** men everywhere to repent" (Acts 17:30).
Thus St. Peter: "The Lord is...**not willing that any should perish** but that all should come to repentance" (2 Peter 3:9).
Thus St. John: "If **any** man sin, we have an advocate with the Father...and he is the propitiation for...the sins of the whole world" (I John 2:1-2).

Sermon: "Free Grace"
April 26, 1739

CHAPTER 2: Fundamental # 1
Methodists are Arminians: What is That?

"I urge that... prayers be made for everyone, even kings in high places....
This is right and acceptable in the sight of God our Savior who desires
everyone to be saved and to come to the knowledge of the truth."
—I Timothy 2:1-4

Jacob Arminius (1560-1609) was a Dutch Calvinist who became a dissenter to the Calvinist notion of predestination. Methodists are Arminians, yet to many of us, that has no real meaning! We believe that God is all-powerful in sovereignty, but we differ from the Calvinists in how God expresses God's providential power. We believe God chooses to express total sovereignty with total love for every one of God's children. Arminius — and Susanna Wesley in a letter to John at Oxford — insisted that we must distinguish between God's foreknowledge and God's predestination. For God to know what choice we will make does not pre-empt our freedom to choose.

The word for this is "synergism." Randy Maddox at Duke Divinity School calls synergism "responsible grace." That is, we must respond to God's grace. Our response must "sync" with God's love. In William Paul Young's best-selling novel *The Shack,* God says to the protagonist Mack:

> True love never forces. Let's say it takes forty-seven life situations and events before you actually hear me. When you don't hear me the first time, I am not frustrated. That first time will be a building block to construct a bridge of healing that one day you will walk across.[1]

Arminianism is the paradigm for Methodist grace theology. According to Wesley scholar Richard Heitzenrater of Duke Divinity School, Wesley decided to meet the Calvinist challenge head-on in November 1777 by producing a monthly magazine himself. Until the

20th century, every Methodist was pretty clear on what it means to be an Arminian. Wesley's distribution of "The Arminian Magazine" popularized the work of Jacob Arminius for over a century. Heitzenrater says Wesley knew Arminianism would offend some, but "was confident that ninety-nine in a hundred persons in England rejected absolute predestination and would thus not take offence."[2]

Christianity Today magazine recently had an image of John Calvin on the front cover with the headline, "John Calvin: The Comeback Kid." The magazine is correct; Calvinism dominates the neo-evangelical movement today. *Time* magazine ranked Calvinism third in its list of the Top 10 forces changing the postmodern world. Rick Warren popularized Calvinist theology in his bestseller, *The Purpose Driven Life*:

> Your parents may not have planned you, but God did. Long before you were conceived by your parents, you were conceived in the mind of God. God custom made your body just the way he wanted it. Many children are unplanned by their parents, but they are not unplanned by God. Your parents had just the DNA that God wanted to make you. He planned the days of your life in advance, choosing the exact time of your birth and death.[3]

Although Warren's book is apparently this generation's classic on the meaning of life in God's grand design, we Arminians do not accept his theology, which is called "monergism" — God is the sole agent in every human event.

To quote God from *The Shack* again, we see a clear picture of Arminianism in the context of bad things happening and Mack's protestations of his little daughter's murder. In an expression of good Arminianism, God says to Mack:

> Don't ever assume that my using something for good means that I caused it or that I need it to accomplish my purposes.

Just because I work incredible good out of unspeakable tragedies doesn't mean I orchestrate the tragedies. Grace does not depend on suffering to exist, but where there is suffering, you will find grace.[4]

In the acronym "TULIP," which summarizes Calvinist theology, the "T" stands for "Total Depravity." Theologian Albert Outler says that from the image of God in which we were created, "Something has gone fearfully awry in the human enterprise." The heart of the human problem is the problem of the human heart. Yet Outler humorously notes, "we believe in total depravity, but not in tee-total depravity!" We Arminians believe that while we are all sinners estranged from God, we can still hear the whispers of God's spirit. In St. Paul's words, "God's Spirit touches our spirits and confirms who we really are. We know who he is and who we are — Father and children" (Romans 8:28, *The Message*). God's love is a "hound of heaven" seeking love. If we listen to our soul, we can "hear" the "still small voice" of God calling us.

Calvinists also believe in what they call "unconditional election" — the "U" of TULIP — that we are elected to be saved or lost, regardless of what we do with our lives. The corollary to this is Jesus' "limited atonement" (the "L") — that Jesus died only for those whom God elected to be saved. We Arminians believe instead that Jesus' atonement was not limited; Jesus died for every person, with no regard for gender, personal features, or "tribe." God's mission is defined in John 3:16: "God so loved the world that God gave his only Son that *whosoever* believes in him will have eternal life." That crucially important word "whosoever" means no limits; and whatever I have done with my life, "whosoever surely means me."

The "I" in the acronym stands for the Calvinist belief that grace is "irresistible." Arminians, on the other hand, believe that grace *is* resistible. God chooses to express his sovereignty with love, not power. God's love, like parental love, limits God's power at one point

23

— what John Wesley calls "human liberty." That is, we have the free will to resist God's grace. Grace is the divine initiative to all; faith is the human response of those who so choose. Let us be careful to quote Paul correctly: "We are saved by grace through faith." The clue to the parable of the Prodigal Son's salvation is, "He came to himself and said, 'I will rise and go to my father…'" The father had been waiting by the gate for years, but respected his son's human liberty enough to allow the boy to "come to himself." The son did not save himself; he realized his father's love.

The "P" in the Calvinist acronym "TULIP" means "perseverance of the saints." The common parlance for this has been "once saved, always saved." Calvinists do not believe we can backslide; we reject that doctrine. Arminians believe that human nature being what it is, we can and do let our relationship with God atrophy and go dormant. Salvation is a dynamic relationship, not a "once upon a time" *fait accompli*. Being a Christian means "walking the walk" with Jesus as the "pioneer and perfecter of our faith." To prevent backsliding, we need to search the Scriptures, pray, take Communion, attend worship, and have spiritually healthy relationships.

CHAPTER 3: Fundamental # 2
"Way of Salvation" Begins With God's Character — Love

"…God is love"

— I John 4:8b, 16

"Thy darling attribute I praise, which all alike may prove,
The glory of Thy boundless grace, Thy universal love."

— Charles Wesley

All other major religions begin with a good man; in Christianity alone the salvation journey begins with a good God! The invulnerable evidence is that we are called to a relationship with God who in Jesus Christ showed Himself a God of redeeming love. The God who is revealed in Jesus inseparably unites the incarnation and the atonement. The God-sent mission of the Bethlehem baby whose birth the angel announced as "good news of great joy which shall be to all people" is the same as the Savior of all humankind who died on the Cross. As Isaac Watts wrote, "Did ere such love and sorrow meet or thorns compose so rich a crown *[as we see]* sorrow and love flow mingled down?"

Millions of tracts distributed with what fundamentalists call "God's Plan of Salvation" typically begin with "You are a sinner." The first Scripture quotation is usually Romans 3:23, "All have sinned and come short of the glory of God." But Wesleyans do not use the term "plan of salvation." We use the term "way of salvation." The word "way" implies "journey" or "walk" rather than some word out of corporate culture like "plan." Parents don't have a plan for their children; they have a relationship. God created us for relationship with Him. As William Paul Young's God says in *The Shack*, "The God who is — the I am who I am — cannot act apart from love!"[1]

Why We Are Not Calvinists

The great debate between Arminianism and Calvinism is not how a sovereign God can love, but how a loving God can be omnipotent. To re-brand Methodism with its historic message, we must define the nature of God's sovereignty. To the Calvinist, God expresses God's sovereignty in his omnipotence, his power. To the Calvinist, every human being is so totally depraved and deserving of eternal damnation that if justice is served, everyone goes to hell. To the Calvinist, God's sovereignty is expressed by "elective grace." The elect are saved; the rest get what they deserve — damnation.

That was the controversy in Wesley's day; that is the controversy that is fermenting anew in the 21st century. Is the nature of God inherently justice or inherently love?

Jerry Walls, professor of philosophy of religion at Asbury Seminary, describes our issue with Calvinism:

> It doesn't do justice to the character of God revealed in Scripture. It does not accurately portray the Holy One who is 'compassionate and gracious, slow to anger, abiding in love' (Psalm 103:8), the God for whom love is not merely an option… but who is such that his eternal nature is to love.[2]

Randy Maddox adds to that,

> The character of God and God's mode of relating to human beings was always at stake in his debates with the Calvinists. He insisted that God was not a despot who arbitrarily chose some for life and others for death. God's relation to humanity was expressed in Jesus Christ… 'Whosoever will may come' was the repeated theme.[3]

The Methodist fundamental doctrine, then, is that God is inherently love. Wesley's sermon, "Free Grace," preached in 1739 at Bristol, was published to refute Calvinism.[4] It begins "How freely does God love the world! While we were yet sinners, 'Christ died for the ungodly… and how freely with him does he 'give us all things'! The grace or love of God, whence cometh our salvation, is free in all and free for all."

Wesley then asks the tough question, "But is this grace free for all, as well as in all?" He then defines what he sees as the essence of Calvinism: "By virtue of an eternal, unchangeable, irresistible decree of God, one part of mankind are infallibly saved and the rest infallibly damned; it being impossible that any of the former should be damned or that any of the latter should be saved."[5]

He then concludes, "If this be so, all preaching is in vain." He calls predestination "a flat contradiction, not only to the whole scope and tenor of Scripture, but also to those particular texts which expressly declare, 'God is love.'" He quotes Psalm 145:9: "The Lord is loving unto *every* man and his mercy is over *all* his works." He refers to God's revelation to Peter that "God shows no partiality" as Peter was called to preach to Cornelius.

Then Wesley rolls out a litany of scriptural references to Jesus' death for "all," for "every man," for the "whole world." He refers to Jesus' invitation, "Come to me all you who labor and are heavy laden, and I will give you rest." He says if that weren't true, all references to God's weeping would be "crocodile tears, weeping over the prey which were doomed for destruction."[6]

Acknowledging that the Calvinists have their own scriptural proof texts, Wesley adroitly admits that he does not know the full meaning of texts like "God hardened Pharaoh's heart." Then he adds:

> There are many Scriptures the true sense whereof neither you nor I shall know till death is swallowed up in victory. But this I know, better it were to say it had no sense at all than

to say it had such a sense as this. It cannot mean, whatever is meant besides, that the God of truth is a liar. No Scripture can mean that God is not love, or that his mercy is not over all his works. This is the blasphemy for which (however much I love the people who assert it), I abhor the doctrine of predestination.[7]

"'Tis Love, 'Tis Love, Thy Name is LOVE"

The first word in the way of salvation is not about us at all; the first word is the character of God — love. The second is that God's love is a seeking, pro-active love. The universal sin of which Romans 3:23 speaks comes third! The word "fall" implies that we once enjoyed a higher level of relationship and spirituality. Wesley uses the term "original righteousness" and therefore sees salvation as restoration or healing. In the words of Wesley's commentary, we have "fallen short of God's image for us."[8]

In the Garden of Eden story, we were made in the image of God — love of God and each other, harmony in all relationships including all creation, and a consequent *shalom,* "full and complete peace." When Wesleyanism fleshes that out, we call it "grace theology," and we must teach it as faithfully as Jews teach the Torah! It is here that we discover and define the core "fundamental" of our belief: God is love. Gilbert Rowe of Duke Divinity School wrote: "Methodism learned and proclaimed the great truth that God deals directly with every [person] and is ready to impart to each one the best of all news — namely, that our sins are forgiven and each of us is a child of God."[9]

In his *Explanatory Notes Upon the New Testament,* Wesley's comments on I John 4:8 are noteworthy. Here in the writings of John the Elder is the Bible's only formal definition of God: "God is love." The Notes read:

This little sentence brought St. John more sweetness, even in the time he was writing it, than the whole world can bring.

God is often styled holy, righteous, wise, but… as He is said to be love intimating that this is His darling, His reigning attribute, the attribute that sheds an amiable glory on all His own perfections.

Wesley says about I John 4:19 — "We love Him because He first loved us" — that "This is the sum of all religion, the genuine model of Christianity. None can say more. Why then should they say less, or less intelligibly?" In Charles Wesley's epic poem/hymn, "O Come Thou Traveler Unknown," we find this Methodist fundamental expressed so poignantly:

> …Who I ask thee, who art thou?
> Tell me thy name and tell me now…
> wrestling I will not let thee go
> till I thy name, thy nature know…
>
> Speak, or thou never hence shall move,
> *and tell me if thy name is love*
>
> 'Tis Love! 'tis Love! Thou diedst for me,
> I hear thy whisper in my heart,
> The morning breaks, the shadows flee,
> pure Universal Love Thou art;
> To me, to all, thy mercies move —
> thy nature and thy name is Love."[10]

In John Wesley's "Sermon on the Mount VI," he says of the opening line in the Lord's Prayer, "If he is a Father, then he is good, then he is loving to his children." He describes God as "our Father who day by day sustains the life he has given; of whose continuing love we know and every moment receive life and breath and all things. So much more boldly let us come to him, and 'we shall find mercy and grace to help in time of need.' (Hebrews 4:16)… We pray because we love, and we "love him because he first loved us'" (I John 4:19).[11]

Bishop Scott Jones cites Wesley's commentary on I Timothy 1:15 and

John 3:16 in his sermon, "The Way to the Kingdom": "The substance of all is this, 'Jesus Christ came into the world to save sinners,' or 'God so loved the world that he gave his only begotten Son, to the end we might not perish, but have everlasting life" (John 3:16). Importantly, John continues, "Indeed, God did not send the Son into the world to condemn the world, but in order that the world might be saved through him."[12]

God's love is neither elective nor selective; it is for all. Wesley's central thrust refers to Jesus' words, "If any man thirst, let him come to me and drink" (John 7:37). He loves one of the latest written of all New Testament verses, "the Lord is not willing that any should perish, but that all should come to repentance" (II Peter 3:9). He closes the sermon with a long hymn from Charles, "Universal Redemption." One line is "Come freely come, whoever will, and living water take." Charles also expresses this in his invitational hymn: "Come sinners to the gospel feast, let every soul be Jesus' guest/ Ye need not one be left behind for God hath bid all humankind."[13]

"For Wesley, grace is the manifestation of God's love,"[14] Bishop Jones wrote. Over and over again, Wesley insisted that John 3:16 is foundational, and he placed this verse in tandem with John 4:9-10: "God's love was revealed among us in this way: God sent his only Son into the world so that we might live through him. In this is love, not that we loved God, but that he loved us and sent his Son.… A few sentences further John the Elder reminds us, "We love because he first loved us" (I John 4:19).

Rick Warren sounds like an Arminian when he writes, "God wants us to run to him, not from him. In fact 365 times in the Bible, God says, '*Don't be afraid.*' That's one 'Fear not' for every day of the year!"[15]

Arminians, like Calvinists, believe in the sovereignty of God. The difference is that Arminians believe God chooses to express God's omnipotence through love more than through power. Wesley insisted that the capstone of being created in the image of God is being endowed by God with human liberty. When love is so thoroughgoing that it sets the loved one free, its power is compromised. In our freedom we can reject God's love. So love is a risk; love is vulnerable. In any relationship, divine or human, when love is rejected the initiator of love must make a decision — to continue loving or to withdraw love. In other words, human love is conditional — "I will love you if…" or "I will love you so long as…" but God's love is steadfast, unconditional, and never-ending.

The love of God is portrayed poignantly in Jesus' parable that German theologian Helmut Thielicke correctly insisted should be called "The Parable of the Waiting Father." When Rembrandt was an old man, he painted his famous "Return of the Prodigal Son," an amazing revelation of the parable's deeper meaning. The central figure is not the son who has returned home, nor the sulking elder brother in the shadow. Rather it is the father, still wealthy as the red robe depicts, but now old and blind. The left hand is the strong clasping hand of a male; the right hand is the caressing hand of a woman! These were the hands that in love never let the boy go.

Rembrandt's painting gives no resemblance of a courtroom where justice is to be administered, or a mediator's desk where a deal is to be struck. The picture portrays nothing of a paternal lecture about bad behavior, immoral relationships, or squandered inheritance — or a demand that the son be willing to "obey the rules of the house" if he is re-admitted. Rather there is an overwhelmingly warm and loving welcome. As one studies the picture, the Scripture seems to appear before one's eyes: "My son who was lost is found. Put shoes on his feet and rings on his fingers and a robe on his shoulder. Kill the fatted calf." Henri Nouwen's book, *Return of the Prodigal Son*, tells how the author's study of this picture changed his ministry and his life.

The same chapter of Luke that records the parable of "The Waiting Father" tells us, "There will be more joy in heaven over one sinner who repents than over ninety-nine righteous persons who need no repentance" (v.7). Maddox helps us see that Wesley's language about salvation is more therapeutic than juridical. Calvinism makes redemption sound like a courtroom where some are punished and some are acquitted; Wesley makes redemption more like a clinic where all the sick are being treated for healing. This does not mean that sin is psychological; it means that sin is what Wesley calls a disease.

Far too many of God's children have lost their way in life. For some, that lostness has led to behavior they cannot change, substances they cannot kick, relationships they cannot break, habits they cannot overcome, and guilt they cannot shake. For some, life has simply lost its meaning. When we have lost our way, we cannot get home alone. Even the best of psychological counseling cannot do what a manifestation of the love of God can do. Warren is right in that God has a purpose for every life — happiness, joy, peace, and some fulfilling relationships. But his emphasis is on what God expects me to do: measure up, change, overcome, resist.

We Methodists insist that Jesus died to show us how much God loves us. As William Paul Young writes in *The Shack*:

> …my purposes are not for my comfort, or yours. My purposes are always and only an expression of love. I purpose to work life out of death, to bring freedom out of brokenness and turn darkness into light. What you see as chaos, I see as fractal. All things must unfold, even though it puts all those I love in a world of horrible tragedies — even the one closest to me.[16]

The character in the book responds, "You are talking about Jesus, aren't you? What did he accomplish by dying?" God answers, "The substance of everything that love purposed from before the foundation of Creation.… Reconciliation is a two-way street and I have done my part. It is not the nature of love to force a relationship but it is the nature of love to open the way."[17]

For Wesley, salvation as a process begins with God's gracious, seeking love:

"If we take this in its utmost extent it will include all that is wrought in the soul by what is frequently termed 'natural conscience,' but more properly, 'preventing grace'; all the 'drawings' of the Father, the desires after God, which, if we yield to them, increase more and more; all that 'light' wherewith the Son of God 'enlighteneth everyone that cometh into the world,' showing every man 'to do justly, to love mercy, and to walk humbly with his God."

Sermon: "The Scriptural Way of Salvation"

*"You are in the hands of a wise Physician, who is lancing your sores in order to heal them. He has **given** you now the **spirit of fear** but it is in order to the **spirit of love and of a sound mind**. You have now **received the spirit of bondage**. It is now the forerunner of the Spirit of Adoption. He is now afar off. Look up! And expect him to cry in your heart, 'Abba, Father!' He is nigh that justifieth."*

— a Wesley letter to a seeker

CHAPTER 4: Fundamental # 3 Preparing Grace — God's Love is a Seeking Love

"There is joy in the presence of the angels of God over one sinner who repents."

—Luke 15:10

In Genesis 1:27, we see that God created us in God's own image, in perfectly harmonious relationship. Then in the creation story of Genesis 3 we read of the "fall" and the subsequent estrangement, alienation, and brokenness of this Creator-creature relationship. Sin is real and deep and destructive, but God never gives up on us!

Wesley did not minimize the pervasiveness of original sin, but as Wesley Theological Seminary professor Lovett Weems writes: "Sin is not what God wants for us. God is not content for us to experience nothing but the seductive pull of original sin. So God, even in our sinfulness, comes to us in grace."[1] As we sing our faith, we say that God comes to us in a "love that will not let me go; I rest my weary soul in thee."[2] God seeks us before we seek God. In Charles Wesley's account of his own journey, he says, "I heard thee whisper in my heart." God's grace is manifest to us before we have a consciousness of God's love for us, or any desire to follow Jesus. We cannot save ourselves. Paul says, "We cannot pray 'Jesus is Lord' except through the power of the Holy Spirit" (I Corinthians 12:3).

This first evidence of grace is what Wesley called "prevenient grace." It is "the grace that comes before," or "preparing grace." The Methodist Article of Religion #VIII speaks of prevenient grace: "We have no power to do good works… without the grace of God by Christ preventing us [*"preparing us"*]. As Weems teaches us: "God comes to us first. Before we ever take a step, God is there.

Within every life, from the beginning, is this simple, basic, elemental initiating presence of God."[3]

This prevenient grace is entirely the work of God: God initiates; we respond. Author Steve Harper points out, "Prevenient grace is to some a novel idea, but it is crucial in understanding Wesley's order of salvation."[4] Wesley called it "the awakening of the soul." This is grace "whispering to our heart," awakening our deadened natural conscience, which Wesley believed "is more or less uneasy when we act contrary to the light of our own conscience."[5]

I had the privilege of sitting under the teaching of British Methodist Rupert Davies, an expert in the mind and soul of Wesley, and heard him say what later appeared in his book: "The relentless teaching about sin is alleviated by the consideration that fallen man still has the law of God written on his heart and a conscience with which to discern it."[6] Davies then gave us three aspects of prevenient grace: conscience, reason, and freedom. All of these played a pivotal role in the development of Wesleyan theology, and all lead us to very different conclusions about God's grace than does Calvinism.

In prevenient grace, Wesley is insisting that the image of God in which we were created is not totally obliterated. Salvation begins with God's loving, seeking initiative, even while we are still "dead in sin." In his sermon "The Image of God," Wesley preached from Colossians 3:10, "Yet our merciful, though rejected, Creator would not forsake even the depraved work of his own hands, but provided for him, and offered to him a means of being renewed after the image of him that created him."[7]

The United Methodist *Book of Discipline* includes prevenient grace in its lists of "distinctive Wesleyan emphases": "This grace prompts our first wish to please God, our first glimmer of understanding concerning God's will, and our 'first transient conviction' of having sinned against God."[8] This seeking love or prevenient grace is clearly an activity of God, but we can resist, refuse, and stonewall it. We can, in the words of an older Methodist generation, "quench the Spirit."

As is so movingly portrayed in Holman Hunt's painting of "Christ at the Door," God's seeking love is seen in Christ knocking at the door, but the latch is on the inside. "With him who opens the door, I will come in and dine" (Revelation 3:20). We are not saved by our faith, but by God's grace through a faith that grace kindles, through a quickened conscience that amazing grace awakens. God's love is relational, and relationship requires two! To God's prevenient, nudging, whispering grace we can say "yes," or "maybe later," or "no." Grace is resistible; here we differ again from the Calvinists.

Asbury Theological Seminary professors Jerry Walls and Joseph Dongell created a novel piece of fiction that provides a picture of the God-initiated dimension of prevenient grace in contrast to Calvinism's concept of elective grace.[9] They picture a prisoner held by terrorists for a long time in a dank cell. She has succumbed to the "Stockholm syndrome" and identified with her captors to the point that she makes no attempt to escape. Only an invasion from outside will rescue her.

The Calvinist view of divine invasion is simple: God invades the camp, swoops up the prisoner, strips off her shackles and blindfold, and makes her free, even though she does not want freedom. The rescuer is irresistible; she is freed against her will. God has been the lone actor throughout.

The Arminian view of the same scenario believes that God steals into the prison and makes it to the bedside of the prisoner. God begins to ask, "Do you know who you are? Let me tell you. Do you know what has happened to you as your captors have made you feel at home in this dark, dank cell?" Let me tell you." Truth begins to dawn. The Savior holds up a mirror and shines a light in it and she sees her sunken eyes and matted hair and frail body. God says, "Do you see what they have done to you and have you have forgotten who you really are? Can I show you a picture of who you really are and what a great restoration to freedom and abundant life if you come with me?"

The Rescuer presses on. "I know a part of you suspects that I have come to harm you, but let me show you my hands. See this blood. I crawled through an awful tangle of barbed wire to get to you. I want to carry you out of here right now. Trust me. Put your arm around my neck and surrender yourself to me as we get to freedom." She could say, "No," but she responds to this seeking, rescuing care, puts her arm around his neck, and welcomes being carried from captivity to freedom.

This little drama portrays so well that we have been captured by sin and developed a comfort zone in our imprisonment. God seeks us out, whispers in our soul, and awakens us to the reality of our circumstances. Like the prodigal son who "came to himself," we do not resist rescue from bondage.

In Disney's "Lion King," Mufasa, the king of the lions, is killed, and his rightful heir, Simba, is cheated out of his inheritance. Simba is transported through the land of the evil hyenas to the culture of the warthogs. Here the lion king is unwittingly comfortable in his new environment. Finally, Rafiki rescues Simba and tells him that he is not a warthog. Rather he is the son of the great Lion King Mufasa! He teaches Simba what it means to be the king of the jungle. He takes the young lion up to a rock ledge overlooking the vast jungle — Simba's rightful kingdom. Then comes the punch line from Rafiki: "Simba, you are more than you have become." That is precisely what the Holy Spirit says to us in prevenient grace!

In Wesley's sermon "Witness of the Spirit I," he stressed the priority of the Spirit's prevenient and direct witness as the necessary precondition to forgiving grace or "blessed assurance of knowing one's sins forgiven." Again, the bottom line is that prevenient grace is divine initiative, witnessing to us that we need not remain in bondage to sin. Logically, the sermon is based on Romans 8:16 — "The Spirit itself beareth witness with our spirit that we are children of God." The implication is profoundly important. Regardless of our sin, our addictions, or the number of people we have hurt; God loves us and is proactively "whispering to our heart" that we are more than we have become.

There is so much good in what Rick Warren writes in *The Purpose of Christmas,* an example being:

> You were created as an object of God's love. He made you in order to love you. Every time your heart beats and every time you take a breath, God is saying, 'I love you.' He loves you when you don't feel his love as much as when you do. He loves you regardless of your performance, your moods, your actions, or your thoughts. His love for you is unchanging.[10]

Unfortunately, Warren immediately follows this beautiful insight with a brief return to his doctrine of predestination!

Prevenient grace also makes humankind morally responsible. That is, we can accept or resist the "still, small voice," the urge to repent, the mystical moment when God seems so near. That response is what Randy Maddox of Duke Divinity School names "co-operant grace." That is, we make a decision, a decision rooted in our God-given human liberty or free will. Because we are free to make the choice of our preference, it is moral. Perkins' William Abraham puts it so accurately: "Prevenient grace is the initial help God gives to everyone to see how grim things are and to form the first intention to get help."

God's seeking love has three dimensions. First, God gave us what Wesley called a "natural conscience." Wesley says of conscience, "Its main business is to excuse or accuse, to approve or disapprove, to acquit or condemn." He interprets St. Paul's understanding of conscience as "a faculty or power, implanted by God in every soul that comes into the world or perceiving what is right and wrong in his own heart and life, in his tempers, thoughts, words, and deeds." Wesley explains that heathens are to be judged on the conscience that is universally "written on their hearts," but "the Christian rule of right and wrong is the Word of God…. This is the lantern for a 'Christian's feet' and a light in all his paths."

Secondly, prevenient grace brings us under conviction for our sin (a state) and our sins (the total package of our thoughts, words, and deeds). Every person has a *kairos* moment, a "God moment" if you will, in which our past rolls by us like an old movie, our present state is a posture of "I'll do it my way," and we have some fear of what is going on with us. In the old days, this was called "coming under conviction." It meant a moment of soul truth. This is the work of the Holy Spirit. As Abraham says it, God has stepped into everyone's inner life to help us see what is wrong with us and to awaken us to a positive response."[11]

Thirdly, prevenient grace comforts us. In ways we cannot understand, God is with us in our hours of distress, fear, and grief. We are "wiped out." We sense some higher power undergirding us and giving us the courage to "soldier on." We all have seen the poem, "Footprints in the Sand." We protested, "As I look back on my hardest hour, I see only one set of footprints in the snow. God, where were you when I needed you most?" And God says, "That single set of footprints are mine; I was carrying you."

Methodist Ira Sankey, song leader for evangelist Dwight L. Moody in the late 19th century, became acquainted in Scotland with a local poem comparing God's seeking love with the highlands shepherds's determination to never lose a sheep. Poet Elizabeth Clephane related that loyalty to the parable of Jesus in Luke 15. One night Moody preached on that text and for the altar call turned to Sankey and said, "Sing something appropriate." Sankey sat down at the piano, hit an A-flat and began to sing from his soul the words of Clephane's

poem to a tune never before rehearsed nor even created. It was
a miraculous moment. Thousands have come to Christ with this
poignant, moving narrative of God's highly personal, never-ending,
seeking love:

'Lord, Thou hast here Thy ninety and nine,
are they not enough for Thee?'
But the Shepherd made answer 'This of Mine
has wandered away from Me.
And although the road be rough and steep,
I go to the desert to find My sheep'
And all through the mountains, thunder-riv'n,
and up from the rocky steep,
There arose a cry to the gate of heav'n,
'Rejoice I have found My sheep!'
And the angels echoed around the throne,
'Rejoice for the Lord brings back his own!'

Francis Thompson, a Roman Catholic in London's Victorian age, was
a destitute, opium addict for years. He was rescued by a Christian
who reached out to him. Thompson's poem "Hound of Heaven" is so
poignantly descriptive of God's love:

I fled Him, down the nights and down the days;
I fled Him, down the arches of the years;
I fled Him, down the labyrinthine ways
Of my own mind; and in the mist of tears
I hid from Him, and under running laughter.
Up the vistaed slope I sped;
And shot, precipitated . . .
But with unhurrying chase,
And unperturbéd pace,
Deliberate speed, majestic instancy,
They beat—and a Voice beat
More instant than the Feet—
"All things betray thee, who betrayest Me." . . .
How little worthy of any love thou art!
Whom wilt thou find to love ignoble thee,

Save Me, save only Me?…
But just that thou might'st seek it in My arms.
All which thy child's mistake
Fancies as lost, I have stored for thee at home:
Rise, clasp My hand, and come!"
"Ah, fondest, blindest, weakest,
I am He Whom thou seekest!
Thou dravest love from thee, who dravest Me."

Fanny Crosby, a devout Methodist who was blind from childhood, gave us over 8,000 hymns, but none is greater than, "Rescue the Perishing." It was written in 1869, but how contemporary the idiom. Listen!

Tho they are slighting Him, still He is waiting,
waiting the penitent child to receive;
Plead with them earnestly, plead with them gently;
He will forgive if they only believe.
Down in the human heart, crushed by the tempter,
feelings lie buried that grace can restore;
Touched by a loving heart, wakened by kindness,
Chords that are broken will vibrate once more.
Rescue the perishing!

Wesley preached "grace is for all and in all." The Holy Spirit quickens our conscience, whispers to our heart, and awakens our soul. God's is a seeking love that never gives up but never violates our human liberty to resist love.

CHAPTER 5: Fundamental # 4
Sin is real — The Evidence is Clear!

"All have sinned and fallen short of the glory of God."

—Romans 3:23

As God stepped onto the stage of human history through the Incarnation, we have seen this as true to God's character: "God so loved the world that God gave… that we might have eternal life" (John 3:16). Now we must ask, "Just what kind of mess did God come into?" This brings us to the doctrine of "original sin" or "birth sin." Though we disagree with those who say that our sinful state is "No. 1," we also disagree with those who do not see the seriousness of sin. In the 1930s, while liberal theology was still strong among theological faculties, Edwin Lewis wrote: "Christian truth has a certain organic character. Change anywhere affects change everywhere. Is it that they want the old terms dropped because they have ceased to believe in what those terms represent?"[1]

First, let's be clear about the "signs of the times" in which Wesley developed his theology of grace. The universities were dominated by the philosophy known as "The Enlightenment." A host of brilliant men updated much of Greek philosophy that, in Outler's words, "was a cherished conviction that men, once freed from their superstitious errors, would recover their innate moral virtue, viz. the power to will the good and to do it."[2] Wesley says: "Accounts of this kind have particularly abounded in the present century.… Here not a few persons of strong understanding and extensive learning have employed their utmost abilities to show what they termed 'the fair side of human nature.'[3] If their accounts of him be just, man is 'a little less than God.' So it is now quite unfashionable to talk otherwise, to say anything disparaging about human nature.'"

Wesley then asks, "In the meantime, what must we do with our

Bibles? For they will never agree with this."[4] This documents that Wesley was reading the literature of the Enlightenment — a philosophy that would later erode the doctrine of original sin in Methodist Sunday school literature; in the social sciences of psychology, sociology, and economics; and in the public school curricula.

But Wesley demurred. As Outler put it, "Something has gone fearfully awry in the human enterprise."[5] This affects every aspect of our theology. Bishop Kenneth Carder explains:

> Sin has deeper roots than personal choices. This disease of the soul — sin — infects all human beings. It invades every aspect of life. Its power exceeds human strength and cannot be defeated by will power. Demonic forces pervade institutions, individuals, cultures, and systems. We fall victim to their prey without realizing it. The insidious powers of sin and death assault humanity with weapons of deceit, treachery, coercion, manipulation, and violence. The results are the persistent distortion of the divine image in humanity…[6]

Wesley insists that the doctrine of original sin is what separates Christianity from all other religions. His text for the "Original Sin" sermon is Genesis 6:5, which ends, "and that every imagination of the thoughts of his heart was only evil continually." Wesley's comment on that verse is, "Allow this and you are so far a Christian; deny it, and you are but a heathen still."[7]

If we are not sinners, we need no salvation! But we are sinners; our predicament is that of Paul in Romans 7 — Is there no one who can do anything for me? That is the real question (Romans 7:24, *The Message*).

We now understand sin to be much more pernicious and pervasive than we did in former generations. When the doctrine of sin was thundered from every pulpit and sermons instilled guilt more than they proclaimed grace, most sin was identified in very personal terms. It was also defined by the morality code of Victorian Puritanism. Even the cultural definition of preaching became a lecture on personal misbehavior — thus the saying, "Don't preach at me." United Methodist seminary faculties in the late 20th century typically moved sin to the level of societal prejudices, systemic evil, and "tribal" prejudice. Many efforts have been and are being made to remove these injustices.

In his sermon "Original Sin," Wesley preached, "So long as men remain in their natural blindness of understanding, they are not sensible of their spiritual wants… " Wesley says we can "acknowledge [God's] being, but have no acquaintance of Him. We can know there is an emperor of China, yet we do not know him."[8] Wesley means we can have a cognitive belief in God but no personal relationship.

Steve Harper can be our teacher here by eliciting certain salient fundamentals from the whole of Wesley's writings.[9]

> If sin were a 'thing' we could escape it, but because it is an infection, the only option is healing. We cannot try enough, learn enough, worship enough, or do enough good works to heal ourselves. Outside help is the only possible solution. The problem of sin infects the very nature of what it means to be human. Any attempts to remove ourselves from it are only exercises in futility. The solution is transformation, not escape. Wesley can help us out of our futile efforts to treat sin as a 'thing.' He keeps using the term 'disease' and pointing out that the only solution is 'taking the cure.'[10]

According to Wesley, what are the symptoms of sin? Sin makes us dead toward God. It gives us a false sense of security and peace. Wesley said:

The poor, unawakened sinner has no knowledge of himself.

He knows not that he is a fallen spirit. Full of diseases that he is, he fancies himself in perfect health. Bound in misery and iron, he dreams he is happy and at liberty… contented in his fallen state, to live and die without knowing he is made in the image of God, ignorant both of his disease and the only remedy for it…[11]

Wesley in another sermon warns that this "soul death" condition produces evil fruits: independence, pride, vanity, covetousness, lust, anger, envy.[12]

Sin is self-captivity. Thinking ourselves free, we become captives of our own reason, desires, prejudice, cultural blindness, and raw lusts — "prey to our own weaknesses."

Sin is helplessness in the effort to change. Wesley did not believe that the image of God in which we are created is destroyed, but he thought it rendered powerless. Sin has done that to us. Wesley said, "Though he strive with all his might, he cannot conquer; sin is mightier than he."[13] Let us call for a reality check; we cannot pull ourselves up by our own bootstraps — the metaphor itself is ridiculous if one is sinking in quicksand. Our "free will" at this point is impotent. God's grace is essential.

Another dimension of original sin is our judgment of others. Did not Jesus say, "With the judgment you make you will be judged, and the measure you give will be the measure you get." In *The Shack*, Mack is told that his judgment is to become the Judge! He is told:

You have judged many throughout your life. You have judged actions and motivations of others as if you really knew! You have judged the color of skin, body language, and body odor. You have judged history and relationships. You have judged beauty and righteousness by your concepts. By all accounts, you are quite well practiced in the activity.[14]

The Achilles' heel of 19th-century liberalism was looking at human nature through rose-colored glasses. Overlooking the "bent to sinning," liberal theology blamed the environment on everything wrong in society, from personal sin to systemic evil. On the eve of World War II, Edwin Lewis wrote:

> Much that we once called sin we today call by some other name, but changing the name does not change the dire reality itself. Frustrations, inhibitions, maladjustments, nonsocial attitudes — all these new ways of describing the ancient enemy of human peace and happiness in no wise do away with the enemy. St. Paul defined the gospel as "the power of God unto salvation to everyone who believes." The great task of the Church is to connect God's children with that power. The gospel of Christ can actually save human lives and restore them to God. It can enable the drunk to attain sobriety; the thief to be an honest citizen, bring home the prodigal son, rehabilitate broken homes, strengthen weak wills, destroy hate in one's spirit, and create peace in troubled breasts. This is not mere verbalism; it is a sober fact of something that has been taking place for centuries and is still happening today.[15]

United Methodist Bishop Scott Jones points out that Wesley clarifies both voluntary sins (willful transgressions of the law of God) and involuntary sins ("sins of infirmity because they arise either out of our ignorance or our being caught unawares"). Wesley, he adds, also delineates "inward sins": our tempers, thoughts, lusts, and hate. Jones then reminds us that sin goes beyond the individual and infects the cultural. The great contribution of the 20th century to the concept of sin was to broaden it to include society's warped values of racism, sexism, approval of pornography and "dirty jokes," and materialism.[16]

"It is your business to save as many souls as you can."

"By salvation I mean not barely, according to the vulgar notion, deliverance from hell, or going to heaven, but a present deliverance from sin, a restoration of the soul to its primitive health, its original purity, a recovery of the divine nature; the renewal of our souls after the image of God, in righteousness and true holiness, in justice, mercy and truth."

— Wesley

CHAPTER 6: Fundamental # 5 Saving Grace — Co-operant and Resistible

"Since we are utterly incapable of living the glorious lives that God wills, God did it for us! Out of sheer grace he put us in right standing with himself. A pure gift. He got us out of the mess we're in and restored us to where he always wanted us to be. And he did it by means of Jesus Christ… Having faith in him sets us clear."
— Romans 3:21-26 (*The Message*)

In Wesley's sermon "Justification by Faith," he begins by re-telling what we now call the great "meta-narrative" on which the Christian faith is based. We paraphrase Wesley here because until we understand this meta-narrative, the gospel does not "compute" for the post-modern mind. The lack of knowing the over-arching story of the Bible leaves many Methodists easy prey for fundamentalists when they ask the point blank question, "Are you saved?" and if you say that you are, their clincher question is, "When were you saved?"

Wesley on "Justification By Faith"

Wesley preached on the "general ground of this whole doctrine of justification," saying (in my paraphrase): In the image of God was man made. As God is love, so man, dwelling in love dwelt in God and God in him. He was accordingly pure as God is pure. Such then was the state of man in the Garden of Eden — holy, happy, knowing and loving God and in harmony with his wife, children and all the animals of creation. To the law of love, God only gave one prohibition. Man disobeyed that prohibition and ate of the tree of which God commanded him, "Thou shalt not eat of it." Thus by one man sin entered the world and became resistant to God's presence in his heart, insisting, "I'll do it my way." Each of us repeats Adam's mistake and begins "baby steps" toward alienation from God, or even jumps right into a life of rebellion and total estrangement. From Genesis 3 to the angel's appearance to Mary, this was the story of humanity's alienation from God, in spite of the law of Moses and the word of the prophets of whose warnings we read in the Old Testament.

In the fullness of time "God so loved the world that he gave his only Son that whoever believes in him would not perish but have eternal life" (John 3:16). Jesus came as a second common head of humankind, a second general parent and representative of the race. In that role as commissioned by the Father, the Son "bore our griefs," and was "wounded for our iniquities." In Christ, God was reconciling his estranged, alienated children to himself. The consequent story is that "as by the offence of one sin came, by the righteousness of the second came the free gift of justification."

"This therefore is the general ground of the whole doctrine of justification."[1]

Coming to Faith

Those who believe in baptismal regeneration make the statement on the day of the baptism of an infant, "Today, (name) became a Christian." This highly sacramental view of baptism has come into vogue in United Methodist seminaries — and therefore among clergy — only in the last generation. Until the 1970s, Wesley's publication of his father's tract "A Treatise on Baptism" (1758) was considered an anomaly.

Historically in Methodism, baptism was a celebration of prevenient grace, saving for the "age of accountability" a youth's or adult's freedom to respond to God's love affirmatively or negatively. With the advent of confirmation, most emphasis came to be placed on history, creeds, worship, and membership vows rather than the Wesleyan "via salutis" or "way of salvation" which we elicit from Wesley's sermons.

Albert Outler wrote, "The fact is that Wesley had changed his views on this point; his evangelical concern was to separate the 'new birth' from all 'external acts' in order to support his newer emphasis on conversion."[2] As Outler noted, this sermon reflects "revisions of the conventional notions of baptismal regeneration." In the 1748 sermon, "Marks of The New Birth," Wesley preached:

> Baptism is not the new birth. A person may be 'born of water' and yet not be 'born of the Spirit.' Lean no more on the staff of that broken reed, that you were born again in baptism. Who denies that you were born children of God, but you have become a child of the devil; therefore you must be born again.[3]

The sermon "The New Birth" was preached first in 1760, printed in five issues of the "Standard Sermons," and was preached in American Methodism as definitive Wesleyan doctrine until rather recently. In the latter sermon, Wesley roared:

> Was you devoted to God at eight days old and… was you consecrated to God the Father, the Son, and the Holy Ghost? You have defied your baptism a thousand times and you do so still day by day. Be you baptized or unbaptized, you must be born again. Otherwise, it is not possible you should be inwardly holy. Do you say, 'But I attend all the ordinances of God; I keep to my church and sacrament.' It is well you do. But all this will not keep you from hell except you be born again. Go to church twice a day, go to the Lord's table every week, say ever so many prayers in private, hear ever so many sermons… the best that were ever preached; read ever so many good books — still you must be born again. None of these things will stand in the place of the new birth.[4]

The following reflects Wesley's "way of salvation":

The Holy Spirit awakens us to our sin. George Hunter helped us all in pointing out that the purpose of Wesley's outdoor sermons was very different from the American revival meeting. The revival called for instantaneous conversion that night! This gave rise to the question, "When and where were you saved?" Wesley did not ask for a "decision for Christ," to use the term introduced by Billy Graham. Rather he preached for an "awakening of the soul." His effort was to sensitize the person "dead in his sins" to the "whisper in the heart" of the Holy Spirit.

William Abraham puts it this way: "At some point the individual must see what is at stake and look to God for forgiveness; God alone can supply relief to the soul. Coming to faith is not so much making a decision as it is waiting for God."[5] Given the power of sin over us, only God can save us. Wesley used the metaphor of "porch" to describe this convicting work of prevenient grace, taking us to the threshold of saving grace.

Here we differ from the Calvinists who insist that when God elects to save us, grace is irresistible. Wesley considered the crowning dimension of being made in the image of God to be "human liberty." We are not marionettes on the end of a string, nor pre-programmed computer chips; we are free moral agents. The crisis moment comes when we say "yes." We can resist God's gracious offer of salvation, like Governor Felix in Acts 24:25, whose response was "On some more convenient day on thee I'll call." From that verse came an old gospel hymn, filled with pathos, "Almost persuaded… almost but lost." On the other hand, we have options. We, like the "prodigal son" in Jesus' parable, can "come to ourselves" and "rise and go to our Father." We do not have to stay in the pigsty.

Personal response. At this point, we "activate" the role of the seeker—the human response to God's grace. Grace now becomes "co-operant," whether we are a child in confirmation class or a serial killer on death row. Randy Maddox aptly calls this "responsible grace." That is, once our soul is awakened, and we are "under conviction" and convinced of our need for outside help, we can "call upon the name of the Lord." That means a voluntary acceptance of God's saving grace. With all Protestants, Methodists turn to Ephesians 2:8-10: "For by grace you have been saved through faith; it is a gift of God, not of works so that anyone may boast."

Entering the "threshold of saving grace" is not a "cookie cutter" process that is the same for everyone. Simplistic approaches such as "The Four Spiritual Laws" or praying "the sinner's prayer" assume that "one size fits all," but if we look at Jesus' conversations with different persons, we find that he meets them where they are, adroitly addresses their point of need or their blind spot, and initiates a saving, restorative, healing relationship. Some of us accepted Jesus as children with little more catharsis than the song, "Into my heart, into my heart, come into my heart, Lord Jesus." Others of us describe our homecoming to God as "O happy day that fixed my choice."

Harry Emerson Fosdick, giant of liberal Protestantism in the 20th century, defined becoming a Christian as "like crossing a river — near the head of the stream where it requires only a small step across a brook, or at the mouth where it requires a long and arduous swim!" Because of the difference in life ages and stages when we come to Christ, our experience of converting grace is different with each person. We must guard against a lockstep process and remember that Jesus met each person in accordance with her or his personality, life situation, and acute need.

Repentance. Repentance is different from remorse. Remorse is a passive feeling of being sorry. It can lead to depression, despondency, and despair. It is a "woe is me" feeling of inescapable guilt. For Wesley, this is the convicting work of prevenient grace — "a thorough conviction of sin." It is divinely initiated. Repentance, in Greek, is the proactive word *metanoia*, which loosely translated means, "turning around and going the other way." Repentance involves change — in behavior, attitude, and habits of dependency and dysfunctional relationships. Wesley insists that we must repent before we can believe the gospel. We must be cut off from dependency upon ourselves before we can truly depend on Christ. He considered repentance as "an entire change of heart and life."

Faith. We might come to our moment of truth in the emotional music and persuasive altar call of a revival meeting, the quiet of a meditative hour during a weekend retreat, the climax of a week of church camp, the trauma of ICU, or any one of hundreds of scenarios. We might be a child making our first "intentional step of faith" or an adult of any age or station. Like Jesus in his earthly ministry, the Holy Spirit meets us where we are. Whatever the setting and circumstance, some things are critical. This is more than "membership training" in church membership — often all that confirmation class is.

This is so crucial in an adult's leap into experiential grace that we must be analytical. Faith, in Wesley's language is, "a sure trust and confidence that Christ died for my sins, that God loves me." We must remember that Wesley's "way of salvation" is anchored in the character of God as love. In order to trust him, we must internalize this and it is hard to do![6]

William Paul Young in *The Shack* has God saying to the protagonist:

> The real underlying flaw in your life, Mackenzie, is that you don't think I am good. If you knew I was good and that everything — the means, the ends, and all the processing of individual life events — is all covered by my goodness, then while you might not always understand what I am doing, you would trust me. You cannot produce trust just like you cannot 'do' humility. It either is or is not. Trust is the fruit of a relationship in which you know you are loved. Until you know I love you, you cannot trust me.[7]

As Steve Harper points out, it was the "prodigal son's trust in his father's love that gave him the confidence to go home."[8] A major roadblock in trusting God and having faith in God's goodness and love is the Calvinist and cultural theology that has made God's sovereignty and power dominate God's attribute of love. We must then go back to our first fundamental: that our salvation begins with God's character. If we believe God is love, then we can fall into God's arms of mercy and pardon and "hear" Jesus' words: "Come to me all you who labor and I will give you rest. For my yoke is easy and my burden is light." When our seeking soul is honest with God, we encounter a mystery — God's grace gives the seeker the ability to respond.

Wesley preached "The Circumcision of the Heart" — what Outler calls a "landmark sermon" — in 1733 at Oxford and in revised form just after Aldersgate. Wesley said, "The best guide of the blind, the surest light of them that are in darkness, the most perfect instructor of the foolish is faith. All things are possible to him who thus believeth, the eyes of his understanding being enlightened, he sees what is his calling, even to glorify God." He then repeats the "faith as revealed in scripture", and adds, "but likewise the revelation of Christ's unmerited love to me a sinner, assures a confidence in His pardoning mercy, wrought in us by the Holy Spirit"… Confidence whereby every true believer is enabled to bear witness, "I know that my Redeemer liveth… I know he loved me and gave himself for me."[9]

Faith is more than doctrinal belief; it is a heartfelt trust in God. William Abraham wrote, "Vague faith in God as creator will not cut it. Nor will bare assent to the creed of the church be enough."[10] The vows of church membership do not equate faith in Christ. Nor is a series of ethical and moral decisions based on "What Would Jesus Do" sufficient. To be meaningful, this moment must be deeply personal. I call it a God-moment: the deep reached by the Deep! This is similar to Wesley's experience at Aldersgate — to trust in God's love and make the leap of faith, really a surrendering of one's will to the will of God.

Charlotte Elliott was an invalid who was bitter to the point that no nurse could care for her very long. Then she made this leap of faith and wrote about it in lyrics that have called millions to a similar experience:

> "Just as I am Thou wilt receive,
> will welcome, pardon, cleanse, relieve.
> Because Thy promise I believe,
> O Lamb of God, I come, I come."

CHAPTER 7: Fundamental # 6
We Can "Know" Our Sins Forgiven

"All who are led by the Spirit of God are children of God.
When we cry, 'Abba,' 'Papá,' it is that very Spirit bearing
witness with our spirit that we are children of God."

—Romans 8:14, 15b-16

John Wesley was a consecrated man before May 24, 1738. Indeed, he was a holy man. However, he was not a happy man. For over three years, he had seen in the German Moravians something he lacked – the quiet confidence of "knowing" one's sins forgiven. Under the mentoring of Moravian Peter Bohler, Wesley had a defining moment in his spiritual journey. In his words:

> About a quarter before nine as one was reading Luther's preface to Romans where he was describing the change which God works in the heart through faith in Christ, I felt my heart strangely warmed. I felt I did trust in Christ, Christ alone, for salvation, and an assurance was given me that He had taken away my sins, even mine, and saved me from the law of sin and death.[1]

A defining characteristic of Wesleyan faith is called either "witness of the Spirit" or "assurance." Wesley preached two sermons on this, both on the same text and with the same title! He cites the doctrine as a Methodist fundamental by saying, "it more clearly concerns the Methodists… clearly to understand, explain, and defend this doctrine because it is one grand part of the testimony which God has given them to bear to all mankind." It is by his peculiar blessing upon them in searching the Scriptures, confirmed by the experience of his children, that this great evangelical truth has been recovered, which had been for many years well nigh lost and forgotten.[2] Randy Maddox insists that "adoption" is the initiation of Christianity's central goal: "restoring the due relations between God and humanity by uniting forever the tender Father and the grateful, obedient child."[3]

Wesley has his critics about his and Charles' conviction that we can "know our sins forgiven." In his two sermons "Witness of the Spirit…I," he uses three arguments to defend the doctrine, "witness of the Spirit":

A. The scriptural foundation is primary, particularly Paul's words on which the sermons are based. Wesley considers this an objective foundation for the "witness of the Spirit" or "blessed assurance":

> All who are led by the Spirit of God are the children of God. For you did not receive the spirit of fear, but you have received the spirit of adoption. When we cry, 'Abba, Father' it is that very Spirit bearing witness with our spirit that we are children of God, and if children, then heirs, heirs of God and joint heirs with Christ (Romans 8:14-17a)

B. The philosophical foundation for the doctrine is sheer logic: this witness must be antecedent to "holiness of life and heart"; 1) we must love God before we can be holy; 2) we cannot love God before we know God loves us; 3) we cannot know God's love until his Spirit bears witness with our spirit. Thus, logically, the foundation for our "house of faith" is laid in Romans 8:16!

C. The subjective foundation for the "testimony of the Spirit" is, in Wesley's words, "hard to find in the language of men." He sees this witness as one of the "deep things of God." He continues, "I mean an inward impression of the soul, whereby the Spirit of God immediately and directly witnesses to my spirit that I am a child of God, that 'Jesus Christ hath loved me and given himself for me,' that all my sins are blotted out, and I, even I, am reconciled to God."[4]

Charles Wesley, as was his custom, converted his brother's prose to verse:

How can a sinner know his sins on earth forgiven?
How can my gracious Savior show
my name inscribed in heaven?
What we have felt and seen with confidence we tell
And publish to the ends of earth the signs infallible!
We by his Spirit prove and know the things of God,
The things which freely of his love
he hath on us bestowed.
Our nature's turned, our mind transformed
in all its powers,
And both the witnesses are joined —
The Spirit of God with ours.

The context of Aldersgate is important. Wesley had long been dissatisfied with his lack of "assurance of faith." He felt a failure in his short stint as a pastor in Wroote, and his missionary work was conflicted to the point he broke contract and returned in February 1738 to London. He preached in four Anglican churches that spring, only to be told that the vestry did not want him to preach for them again! He walked forty-three miles with Bohler, who was en route from Germany to Georgia with a layover in England. Bohler said, "My brother, my brother, that philosophy of yours must be purged away."[5]

 "Assurance" or "witness of the Spirit" was the missing dimension of John Wesley's spiritual journey before Aldersgate. Until this time, his energies were focused on himself; after this time, his energies were focused on bringing others into the kingdom. In Georgia as a missionary for seventeen months, he worked very hard but his ministry showed little fruit. Furthermore, he had a disastrous romance, and even his regular meetings with the Moravians did not result in "the peace of God which passes our understanding." By the winter and spring of 1738, he was burned out and saw no professional future as an Anglican priest.

Every seeker of experiential grace needs to know that Wesley's long and arduous chapter of faithfulness and near-monastic lifestyle did not bring him what his father Samuel called the "greatest proof of Christianity" — the inward witness. Many a faithful pastor and layperson who has been to church for years and lived a life of impeccable character and careful morality could say with Wesley that "one thing I lack" — the assurance that my sins are forgiven and that "I know the things of God."

Some of us are like John Wesley, in that we spend our childhood in a Christian family and a warm, loving local church, are confirmed at about age twelve, and will always answer in the affirmative if someone asks, "Are you a Christian?" Like Wesley, we live with high standards of morality, ethics, and self-control of what he called "our tempers." And yet we can lack the "knowing God" that he experienced at Aldersgate. We can be a good person, serve on lots of church committees, sing in the choir, and rear a solid family but still have this gnawing emptiness about "converting grace." If this is our sacred journey, we need to take Wesley's advice and "cry out to God" for what Fanny Crosby described as, "Blessed assurance, Jesus is mine/ Oh, what a foretaste of glory divine."

Emotions are slippery. In seminary, I took heart at Wesley's words:

> There may be foretastes of joy, peace, and love — and those not delusive, but really from God — long before we have the witness in ourselves, before the Sprit of God witnesses with our spirits that we have… forgiveness of sins… But it is by no means advisable to rest here. Continue crying to God until his Spirit cry in our heart, 'Abba, Father.' This is the privilege of all children of God.[6]

"Wesley had met God for himself. By 1739 he was beginning to integrate all that he had learned and experienced into a new vision of the Christian tradition."[7] From that, all Methodists take our own cue for our spiritual journey. Our "Aldersgate" often comes after many years of faithful discipleship. We do not have a "God moment" every day or week or month or year. However, when we do, we have a "confidence to tell." Jesus' most common invitation was simple and unexplored: "Follow me." His assurance becomes our assurance, "Whoever comes will in no way be cast out." Of all the revival sermons I ever heard, no message was so encouraging to me as a young man than the message one morning in a summer camp from John 15, verses 14 and 11: "You are my friends... I have said these things to you that my joy may be in you and that your joy may be complete."

Randy Maddox insists that Wesley's preference for the work of the Spirit is "healing." Wesley preached that sin is a disease for which only God has the remedy; therefore we are better served to use terms of the clinic rather than the court! If we think "therapeutic" rather than "juridical," we can see Jesus as the Great Physician healing the "sin-sick soul and making the wounded whole." In this Wesley reveals his adoption of some Eastern Christian (i.e. Orthodox) theology over Augustine and other Western (i.e. Catholic) theologians. Therefore Wesley's desire is for God's grace to empower us with a recovery of the likeness of God. To accomplish this, we need to be freed from the power of sin and empowered by the presence of God. A corollary of this is the emphasis of God's love more than God's sense of justice. That is, Jesus did not die to "buy" our forgiveness; God first loved us and sent his Son to reconcile us to the Father.

This is implicit in the much-debated John 14:6 text, "No one comes to the Father but by me." It does not mean that God does not love every human being equally as his child; rather, it means that no one sees God as "Abba" or "Papa" except through Jesus. To others, God might be creator, judge, and even redeemer, but not relationally intimate! None other than a Christian would sing, "He walks with me and he talks with me and he tells me I am his own." Yes, that refers to Jesus and Mary Magdalene, but Jesus said, "The Father and I are one. If you have seen me, you have seen the Father." Bottom line — Methodism's way to salvation is paved with LOVE![8]

"There is scarce any word in Holy Writ which has given more offense than this — 'Christian Perfection.' The word 'perfect' is what many cannot bear. The very sound is an abomination to them. Hence some have advised to lay aside the use of such expressions. But are they not found in the oracles of God? Whatever God hath spoken; that we will speak."

Sermon: "Christian Perfection"

Wesley insisted that the Spirit of God does not cease working in us after we have experienced God's saving grace:

"God is continually breathing, as it were, upon his soul, and his soul is breathing unto God. Grace is descending into his heart and prayer and praise ascending to heaven. And by this intercourse between God and man, this fellowship with the Father and the Son, as by a kind of spiritual respiration, the life of God in the soul is sustained; and the child of God grows up till he comes to 'full measure of the stature of Christ.'"

Sermon: "The New Birth"

CHAPTER 8: Fundamental # 7
Perfecting Grace —
One Day at a Time, Dear Jesus

"Everyone who lives on milk, being still an infant, is unskilled in the word of righteousness. Solid food is for the mature, for those whose faculties have been trained to distinguish good from evil. Therefore let us go on to perfection…"
—Hebrews 6:1

Ask and you will receive, so that your joy may be complete."
—John 16:24b

There's one thing every Christian has in common—that Jesus has said, "Follow me." I love the words of Albert Schweitzer:

> He comes to us… just as on the shore of the lake He approached those men who knew him not. His words are the same: 'Follow thou Me!' and He puts us to the tasks He has to carry out in our age. He commands. And to those who obey, be they wise or simple, He will reveal Himself in the fellowship of peace and activity, of struggle and suffering, till they come to know, as an inexpressible secret, Who He is…[1]

Colin Williams speaks for the majority of serious Wesley scholars when he wrote, "There can be no doubt of the importance of the doctrine of perfection in the history of Methodism."[2] Wesley wrote in his recap of the rise of Methodism, "…men are justified before they are sanctified; but still holiness was their point. God then thrust them out, utterly against their will, to raise a holy people." He called it "the peculiar doctrine committed to our trust." Wesley considered his doctrine of Christian perfection the "grand depositum" of Methodism. Wesley wrote less than a year before his death that the people called Methodist "were raised up to proclaim this truth."

Bishop Nolan B. Harmon wrote in his classic, *Understanding The Methodist Church*:

> The doctrine of Christian perfection has been the one specific contribution which Methodism has made to the Church universal. In this one doctrine we stand by ourselves and utter a teaching that reaches up fearlessly and touches the very scepter of God's grace. If we can live one day without sin, we can live two, then many. Why not all?[3]

Wesley's problem was how to define a perfection for "imperfects" like us! We must not look at humankind through rose-colored glasses, forgetting creaturely limitations on the one hand and the continuing effects of original sin on the other.

What we mean by Christian perfection is this — we grow in grace, we draw "closer to Thee," until except for constant human frailty and cultural blindness of which we are not conscious, we can live in relational harmony with God. Harry Denman once taught my family at our parsonage breakfast table how he prayed the Lord's Prayer every morning, "Thy will be done — in me, in me — on earth as it is in heaven." To this saintly layman, perfection meant a daily conscious conformity to the will of God as he understood it. This is much of what Wesley meant when he used the term "perfection of the pilgrim." This we today understand in the idiom, "perfecting grace." It is, in Colin Williams' words, "The perfect Christian is holy, not because he has risen to a required moral standard, but because he lives in a state of unbroken fellowship with Christ."[4]

Bishop Earl G. Hunt often told the apocryphal story of the young man who decided to answer negatively when he stood before the annual conference for ordination and was asked, "Are you going on to perfection?" He therefore answered, "NO." A murmur went across the conference, "What would the bishop do?" The wise bishop simply looked at the young rebel and asked, "Then, son, what are you going on to?" Anything short of perfection will be a goal we can reach and look down from our pious pedestal in self-righteousness. If Christian perfection is true to its name, a major characteristic will be humility.

Bishop Harmon and others write categorically, "Wesley never claimed for himself that he had been 'made perfect,' even as he preached it as the goal of the journey."[5] Reflecting Wesley's own caveats, Bishop Harmon wrote, "this experience does not deliver us from the infirmities, ignorance, and mistakes common to man, nor from the possibilities of further sin."[6] The Christian is challenged to "have the mind which was in Christ Jesus" and to respond wholly to the will of God as we understand it, with the result that sin loses both its grip and its appeal. The Holy Spirit consciously becomes our spiritual watchdog through which we examine our soul for sins of thought, word, and deed.

Fifteen months after Aldersgate, Wesley is writing about the rest of one's Christian journey beyond accepting Christ as our personal Savior. He calls it "sanctification." Because that term acquired so much moralistic baggage identified with the "holiness code" of the 19th century, the doctrine's recovery has used the word "perfecting grace." Of this dimension of one's journey, Wesley wrote, "I believe it to be an inward thing, namely, the life of God in the soul of man, a participation of the divine nature, the mind that was in Christ, or, the renewal of our heart, after the image of Him that created us."[7] Robert Cushman insisted that neither the Anglican Articles of Religion, nor Martin Luther, nor John Calvin understood perfecting grace as Wesley did.[8] Wesley searched the Scriptures and found I Corinthians 1:30 and Romans 12:1. Wesley had found in his own experiences in Oxford and Georgia of seeking to be a holy man that holiness is not attainable through self-discipline, but finds it given only and entirely as a gift of the Holy Spirit.[9]

In his sermon "On God's Vineyard," Wesley, in Outler's humorous words, "took a swig of triumphalism"[10]:

Who has wrote more ably than Martin Luther on justification by faith alone, and who was more ignorant of sanctification? How many of the Romish writers have wrote strongly and scripturally on sanctification who were entirely unacquainted with justification? But it has pleased God to give the Methodists a full and clear knowledge of each, and the wide difference between them.[11]

There has probably never been a hymnal among Wesleyans that did not include Charles Wesley's classic, "Love Divine, all love excelling." He was clearly speaking of sanctifying grace:

> Breathe, O breathe thy loving Spirit
> into every troubled breast,
> Let us all in thee inherit,
> let us find that second rest.
> Take away our bent to sinning,
> Alpha and Omega be
> End of faith, as its beginning,
> set our hearts at liberty.

In another hymn, Charles has us sing,

> O, may Thy love possess me whole,
> My joy, my treasure, and my crown;
> Strange fires far from my soul remove;
> My every act, word, thought, be love!

Yet perfecting grace is the most divisive of all Methodist fundamentals. Its proponents first married it to Victorian Puritanism and then immersed it in enthusiasm! Outler reflects on this: "This syndrome of self-righteousness amongst the holiness people led the 'mainstream' to throw the Wesleyan baby of true holiness out with the 'second blessing' bath water."[12] Most were considered fanatics to the point that at the General Conference of 1894, the Episcopal Address of the Methodist Episcopal bishops virtually invited those who would "push' holiness to leave. The result was the founding of the Nazarene Church.

The loss was great because mainline Methodism from that point woefully neglected the essence of Wesley's insistence on "holiness of heart and life." Of the several mergers in the 20th century, there was never an overture to bring back to the mother church those who had left because of either racism or holiness. The sad result was that most Methodists never heard of perfecting grace because most pastors would not touch the subject with a ten-foot pole.

Perfecting grace cannot be omitted as a Methodist fundamental. The question was never deleted from ordination in any branch of Methodism: "Are you going on to perfection?" But what do we mean by this "second work of grace" in the grand scheme of Wesley's "experimental divinity"?

First let us enunciate what Wesley did not mean by Christian perfection:

Christian infallibility. No one possesses absolute knowledge, perfect judgment, consistent performance, or total control of what Wesley called one's "tempers." Wesley called that "angelism," and said he wanted a holiness for real people engaged in real life.

Superiority. Moving deeper into the "mind which was in Christ" must not breed a rank of "first" or "second" levels of status. The effect must be humility, not pride.

Immunity from life's problems. This is a mistake made by those who combined holiness with the charismatic movement of the 1970s and later. Being sick, falling victim to natural law disasters, being wounded or killed in war, being victim to crime, and losing one's job must not be seen as the lack of Christian perfection. It is not, in Steve Harper's words, "vaccination from reality."[13] It is patently not true that "if you have sufficient faith, you will be healed." Christians die at the same degree as everyone else — 100 percent. All those who preach that message end up dying one day, and we trust their death was not caused by a failure of faith.

Instantaneous "faith accompli." One of my teenage memories is hearing people give specific dates for their conversion and their being sanctified. We can certainly have a liberating experience of surrendering to God some habit, relationship, or attitude that has denied the Holy Spirit's empowering us to grow. However, once that block is moved we must "press on to the high calling which is ours in Christ Jesus." The devil is no slacker and we are constantly being tempted in thought, word, and deed.

Two nuances of grammar are theologically important. Wesley spoke of "going on" to perfection more than of having arrived. To claim perfection reflects Pharisaism and sanctimonious spiritual pride. The second grammatical nuance is "perfecting grace." This is in keeping with Wesley's description of the Christian journey as "grace upon grace." Perfecting grace is, in Bishop Ken Carder's words, "a gift [of God] emerging from friendship with and obedience to Christ, a process of maturing in discipleship until the heart is habitually inclined to do what is right. Perfection must never be seen as perfectionism."[14]

For generations, sanctification was maligned by its friends and caricatured by its opponents. It was preached as an instant "second work of grace" received by going to the altar in a revival meeting. The preacher said that while in justifying grace our sins were forgiven, we still retained what the old holiness movement called "carnal nature." In sanctification, one would be baptized by the Holy Spirit and purged of this carnal nature so that henceforth the sanctified would be "spirit filled" and "spirit led." Hillary T. Hudson reflects this in his 1882 edition of *The Methodist Armor*:

> Sanctification brings the whole body, heart, spirit, mind,

family, property, influence, and intellect into captivity to Christ so the Christ thinks for him, puts the love of God in his heart. The sanctified Christian is unselfish and beneficent, a vessel of Christian love, the mind to reflect the glory of God, and one's property to advance the cause of God. Throw yourself into the ocean of divine love, and be filled with all the fullness of God.[15]

 If all this seems personal, it is! For four of my teenage years, I was told that an emotional experience of being made "perfect" would come as a baptism of the Spirit instantaneously. It did not, even though I sought it honestly. In its place, I followed the legalism of the holiness code. I abstained not only from alcohol and tobacco but also from dancing, playing cards, and going to movies. I skipped social celebrations during high school. Then I abandoned the doctrine for many years. For the most part, all of Methodism abandoned it! Because of this painful experience with a distorted version of perfecting grace, I have come to embrace a more recent understanding of Christian perfection as a journey that we walk, enabled by what John Wesley accurately called "means of grace." In my renewed journey of seeking God's perfecting grace, Brian Wren speaks to me in his hymn:

> This is a day of new beginnings,
> time to remember and move on,
> time to believe what love is bringing,
> laying to rest the pain that's gone.
> Christ is alive, and goes before us
> to show and share what love can do.
> This is a day of new beginnings;
> our God is making all things new.

Having admitted that both "holiness code" proponents and "modernist" opponents of Christian perfection did us a disservice, let us renew our insistence that perfecting grace is a Methodist fundamental! Wesley borrowed from a wide and deep stream of piety in his insistence on a goal of "perfect love" and its two-dimensional focus of "loving God and loving neighbor." He says, "This is the sum of Christian perfection: It is all comprised in that one word, LOVE."[16] Perfecting grace is our continuing willingness to "let go and let God" have his wonderful way in our lives. An old gospel hymn, "Higher Ground," had the line,

> I'm pressing on the upward way,
> New heights I'm gaining everyday.
> Still praying as I'm onward bound,
> 'Lord plant my feet on higher ground.'
> My heart has no desire to stay
> Where doubts arise and fears dismay;
> Though some may dwell where those abound,
> My prayer, my aim is higher ground.[17]

In teaching seminary students, I employ Wesley's metaphor of "the porch" as God's convicting grace leading us to repentance, "the door" as our co-operant response of accepting God's love and experiencing justifying grace, and "the house" as God's taking us room to room for the rest of our lives. At "each room" God takes us by the arm and says, "I need to look in this room." We are often resistant and say, "No, Lord, I am not yet ready to let you cleanse and purge that dark stain from my life." Often it is a broken relationship, a nagging guilt, or even a living lie. So God says, "I must go in there. We cannot bypass a skeleton-occupied closet on our way to the pretty parlor." The Holy Spirit continues to whisper to our heart, to nudge our conscience, to lead us to new insights through relationships, readings, and means of grace.

Bishop Carder reminds us that justifying grace is what God does *for* us in the effecting of Jesus' death for the forgiveness of sin, and sanctifying grace is what God does *in* us—holiness in life. These do not affirm human potential as much as the power of God."[18] He also points out our tendency to interpret sin through our provincial cultures; thus, we are blinded and unable "to see ourselves as others see us" (to quote Robert Burns). Sanctification must be seen from a higher plane than parish, region, nation, race, gender, income, and denomination.

Wesley, to his credit, always insisted that sanctification is "love of God and love of neighbor." Walter Muelder has written, "Twentieth century holiness envisages a whole person in a whole society."[19] Reinhold Niebuhr enlightened us on the difficulty of being a moral individual in a society tainted by sin. Presbyterian Scot John Baille acknowledged that Reformation thought does not take seriously enough the possibility of holiness in Christian living. In the late-twentieth century, Methodism recovered Wesley's insistence on "grace upon grace" or perfecting grace, but we also recovered his insistence that there "is no holiness but social holiness."

Bishop Larry Goodpaster has stated our "Methodist fundamental" on personal and social holiness so well:

> Indeed, if we reclaim Wesley, we will reclaim the 'both-and' nature of holiness.… We must say that without social holiness there is no personal holiness, only an assembly of people dreaming of some vague notion of heavenly escape. However… personal holiness precedes social justice activities, for we must have our hearts and soul reconciled, regenerated, justified, and sanctified before we venture forth to serve others, love neighbor, and imitate Jesus. It cannot be reduced to one or the other, but there must be a healthy balance on both sides of holiness.[20]

To grow in grace, to be discipled into the "mind that was in Christ Jesus," Wesley outlined what he called the "means of grace." To those we now turn.

*"By 'means of grace' I understand outward signs, words, or actions ordained of God to be the ordinary channels whereby he might convey to us preventing (**'preparing'**), justifying, and sanctifying grace." I use this expression because I know of none better. We bless God both for the 'means of grace and the hope of glory.'"*

Wesley, as we shall point out, warned that "all these means when separate from the end, are less than nothing and vanity. If they are not conducive to the knowledge and love of God they are not acceptable in his sight…. The great foundation of the Christian building is, 'By grace ye are saved' — free grace, the mere mercy of God through the merits of his well-beloved Son."

"How may one attain thereto? If you say, 'Believe, and thou shalt be saved,' or 'wait on God,' we ask, 'But how are we to wait' According to the Holy Writ, all who desire the grace of God are to wait for it in the means which God hath ordained; in using them, not in laying them aside."

*"Use all the means as **means**; as ordained, not for their own sake, but in order to the renewal of your soul in righteousness and true holiness. My son shall ever be always of the loving-kindness of the Lord…."*

Sermon: "The Means of Grace"

CHAPTER 9: Fundamental # 8
Mr. Wesley's "Means of Grace"

"I pray that, according to the riches of his glory, he may grant
that you may be strengthened in your inner being with power
through the Spirit and that Christ may dwell in your hearts
through faith, as you are being rooted and grounded in love."
—Ephesians 3:16-17

"Religion that is pure and undefiled before God, the Father is this:
to care for orphans and widows in their distress…. What good is
it if you say you have faith but do not have works? Can faith
save you? Faith by itself, if it has no works, is dead."
—James 1:27; 2:14, 17

The term "means of grace" fell into disuse for many years of
Methodist preaching and teaching. For Wesley, these "means" were
not ends in themselves, but were tutors, or spiritual disciplines.
He insisted that they can be God's means of leading us from what
he called "weak faith" to a mature relationship with God in all the
dimensions of our lives – habits, attitudes, relationships, and spiritual
disciplines.

Fundamentalists often glory in citing a moment of being "saved,"
as if that is the sum and summary of being a Christian. For Wesley,
the peace of mind that usually accompanies our repentance and
"knowing our sins forgiven" is just the beginning of the journey.
At that point, he said, we are children in the faith, and that "grace
reigns, but sin remains."[1]

Wesley broke with the Moravians because he insisted that "weak
faith" can be strengthened by the means of grace, which the church
alone supplies. He said, "I believe it is right for him who knows not
faith to go to church, commune, pray, read the Scripture, do all the

temporal good he can and endeavour after doing spiritual good…"[2] By the discipline of these means, we are encouraged to pursue the "high calling which is ours in Christ."

We err to make spiritual discipline into a magic mantra! Wesley, in his sermon "The Means of Grace," warned:

> Before you use any means let it be deeply impressed on your soul: There is no power in this. It is in itself a poor, dead, empty thing; separate from God, it is a dry leaf, a shadow… Settle this in your heart… that there is no power to save but in the Spirit of God… consequently even what God ordains conveys no grace to the soul if you trust not in him alone.[3]

When Wesley spoke of Christian perfection as a dimension of grace theology, his doctrine was always accompanied by his exhortation to "go on" to perfection. See the journey imagery! Let us think of this as a continuing enrichment of internalizing God's love and grace. Being a Christian is no longer centered in the institutional church as the end, but as the means. Fulfillment is not in committees, but in the power of vision and the accompanying presence of God. Secondly, as the late psychologist and author Scott Peck said in the opening line of his book, *The Road Less Traveled*, "Life is difficult." We need more than the distant memory of confirmation or conversion, and participation in traditional classes and committees, to be victorious over trouble.

If we are to grow in "taming our bears," "caging our lions," and knowing our purpose, we must have some spiritual discipline. We can attain the faithful courage to say "no" to sins of the flesh and sins of the spirit that entice us. We can practice the presence of God and see love overcome fear. We can attain a lifestyle that combines responsibility with freedom and freedom with responsibility. Just as Paul said, "I can do all things through Christ who strengthens me," he also said, "without him I can do nothing."

In his 1974 Fondren lectures at Southern Methodist University, Albert Outler morphed his lifetime of scholarly Wesleyan study into a rather folksy presentation. In his last lecture, he summarized Wesley's doctrine of holiness with his logic: "We have faith in order to love, we love in order to be good, we are good in order to be happy—all of which is what God made us for in this world and the next. This is 'holy living' as John Wesley saw it."[4] Outler had identified fifty-four quotes in which Wesley paired "happy" with "holy."

Therefore, I encourage you, dear reader, to practice Wesley's means of grace. Do not fall prey to the cultural mythology that "being spiritual" will make you morbid or a wimp. Christian discipleship empowers us with faithful courage. John Wesley's nerve in facing mobs took courage to match that of Martin Luther King, Jr. His energy is legendary. He had been taught from infancy to hold his emotions in check and he consequently was not psychologically given to exuberance, flippancy, or small talk.

And yet, according to his admirers and critics, Wesley had a strange, insistent reality of cheerfulness, joy, and high spirits. He was, in Outler's words, "a happy man." He died happy: singing, praying, and with the words on his lips, "Best of all, God is with us." We would do well to follow his model of spiritual discipline as a means of conquering many of our human infirmities, channeling our energies into outward works of righteousness, and ending our struggle with unforgiven sins and unresolved guilt.

Therefore, by the mercies of God, John Wesley is a mentor of merit who can lead us to a life well-lived if we learn from what he called living by the "means of grace."

Like many of us, Wesley grew up in the church. Like many clergy, he felt God's call to ordained ministry while he was in college. For thirteen years (1725-38), he read deeply in the writings of saints who urged every Christian to be very disciplined, to practice acts of

Christian mercy, and certainly to "attend the ordinances of God," by which they meant the various ministries of the local church. During this chapter of his life, he practiced what he always called "holiness of heart and life." In this time of his spiritual journey he lacked the assurance of his personal salvation and the "peace which passes understanding." He came to that experience through the mentoring of the Moravians. In Methodism, we still have an interweaving of spiritual discipline and an evangelical experience of God's saving grace. Between the liturgical churches and the evangelistic "free" churches, we are the "church of the middle way."

Eighteen months after the Moravians had "midwifed" Wesley's experience of "knowing his sins forgiven" at Aldersgate, he could no longer abide their doctrine of "stillness." They insisted that until a person had "full assurance of faith," they should not take Communion nor practice any works of mercy. Rather they should "lie still at Jesus' feet" until they had an emotionally cleansing experience of faith. By contrast, Wesley would not negate his years of leading the Holy Club at Oxford, where they ministered to prisoners, organized daycare for children, fed the poor, and insisted, "There is no holiness without social holiness." Wesley insisted that Christianity cannot be a "solitary religion." He insisted that ethics is the fruit of faith, and he abhorred any doctrine that "allows a believer to have a passive attitude toward either the means of grace or the demand of the Gospel for actual righteousness."[5]

Unlike Martin Luther, John Wesley loved the book of James! Methodism has always been known for establishing orphanages, funding missional ministries, founding colleges, sponsoring homes for the mentally challenging, responding to disasters, and ministering with the poor. Therefore Wesley's "means of grace" are the capstone of Methodist fundamentals.

William Abraham helps us clarify that Wesley's first concern was the salvation of souls, but that God had supplied various means for the reception of grace, and most of those means are standard practices of your local church![6] The reality is that for those of us who grew up in Christian homes, went to Sunday school and church, and made early commitments to Christ, the "means of grace" nurtured us in the faith until we, like Wesley, had our own "Aldersgate" experience. This came in an evangelical campus ministry, a summer camp, a retreat like "Walk to Emmaus," a Bible study, or the ICU unit of a hospital!

We must reject those who negate the years of our spiritual journey when we followed Christ "from a distance." Millions of nominal Christians who fill the pews and support the church budgets are "salt of the earth" people who have served faithfully on church committees, kept some modicum of our church vows, and practiced morality as a lifestyle. Of these, Wesley said point-blank to the Moravians, "There are degrees of faith. A man may have some degree of it before all things in him are become new—before he has the full assurance of faith, the abiding witness of the Spirit, or the clear perception that Christ dwelleth in him."[7]

By July 20, 1740, the final break came when the Methodists left the Moravians forever. However, it has only been in the last generation that Methodism recovered Wesley's "means of grace" as a Methodist fundamental. Wesley said conclusively:

> ...there are means of grace, i.e. outward ordinances, whereby the inward grace of God is ordinarily conveyed to man before the faith that brings salvation... One of these means is the Lord's Supper. He who has not faith should wait for it through the use of this and other means by which God hath ordained.[8]

Methodism's sacramental heritage atrophied terribly. Only vivid and spontaneous experiences of grace fill the early testimonials. In recent years, further study of Wesley has shown us that in his own sermon, "The Means of Grace," Wesley recognized that the Church had tragically neglected many of the poor, the disenfranchised, and the "quiet of the land" as well as the drunkards, thieves, and rascals! But then he made the case for the "means of grace" as "outward signs, words, or actions ordained of God to be the ordinary channels whereby he might convey to men preventing, justifying, and sanctifying grace."

Then Wesley listed the means by which we can either be led to "the full assurance of our salvation" or be sustained as we walk the road less traveled to grow through the seasons and experiences of life, a journey which Wesley called "grace upon grace." We consider it therefore a Methodist fundamental that these ordinary channels are often the occasions when we have our "God moments." They are necessary; we need them. Thomas à Kempis once wrote, "I have never found anyone so religious and devout that he had not sometimes a withdrawing of grace or felt not some decrease of zeal."[9]

Using these expressive actions as vehicles for God to convey grace are means by which we respond to God's grace. When a trainer "breaks" a horse, the trainer does not break the horse's will; rather the trainer channels the horse's abilities to a more useful purpose, and indeed, to an almost intimate relationship, as we learn from the techniques of "the horse whisperer." Properly done, the training process fulfills what we understand to be the horse's creative purpose and meaning! It is definitively co-operant and synergistic — the trainer and the horse in mutually responsive relationship. Just so, the undisciplined person might seem to be free, but in reality has no meaning and purpose in life. By God's means of grace, we exchange the heavy yoke of sin for Jesus who said, "My yoke is easy and my burden is light." Discipline is really liberating.

Wesley's Means of Grace

"By 'means of grace' I understand outward signs, words, or actions,
ordained of God… to be the ordinary channels whereby
he might convey to men, preventing, justifying,
or sanctifying grace."[10]

—John Wesley, 1741

Prayer, whether in secret or the great congregation. While it's true that, "Prayer is the soul's sincere desire, unuttered or expressed,"[11] our prayer life is often so "catch as catch can" that we simply forget that we have committed ourselves to intercessory prayer for a sister or brother. What's more, we have allowed prayers of petition to occupy a lion's share of our prayers. Let us practice beginning our prayers with meditation on a recent scene of beauty in creation, or the music of a great choir, or some other reminder of God's majesty.

Then, unless we are in a crisis moment, let us be careful to "count our blessings" before we move to our burdens. Giving thanks for what is should come before complaining about what is not. Let us beware of making God a cosmic errand runner. God does not need us to jog his memory! Intercessory prayer is lifting up persons and concerns and asking God to show us how we can be an "angel of mercy and grace." Our motive for intercessory prayer is concern, not ordering the Almighty to do his homework! Lastly, we need to do our own spiritual housecleaning, asking God to empower us to do what we cannot do alone—to forgive, to have faithful courage, to overcome fear, to "kick" habits, and to trust God as one who loves us.

Because I am a person afflicted with insomnia, I close my nighttime prayer by asking for release from the burdens and stress of the day followed by a slow, meditative recitation of the 23rd Psalm. At the lowest moment of my life, in the winter of 1980, I had a "God moment" as the sun was rising over Kansas City, and I reached that long familiar line: "He maketh me to lie down in green pastures."

I had always concentrated on the green pastures and skipped the predicate! That night/morning I realized that because God loves us, God has to sometimes discipline us. I had to be made to lie down before I could get Don out of the driver's seat and look up to God as the "rod and staff" who would lead me through the valley, deliver me from fear of evil, fill my cup, and anoint my head with the "balm of Gilead" that "makes the wounded whole and cures the sin-sick soul." The 23rd Psalm is my mantra into the awareness of God's presence.

Another dimension of prayer that has become increasingly meaningful for me is the rich mine of prayers from the Church across the ages. I mention here only two. One is a prayer that was in the older Lord's Supper liturgy of The Methodist Church—the "Prayer of Humble Access." The essence of this prayer is "We do not presume to come… trusting in our own righteousness but in Thy manifold and great mercies. We are not worthy so much as to gather up the crumbs under Thy table, but Thou are the same Lord whose nature is always to have mercy.… The other is the "Collect for Purity": "Almighty God, unto whom all hearts are open, all desires known, and from whom no secrets are hid; cleanse the thoughts of our hearts by the inspiration of Thy Holy Spirit, that we may perfectly love Thee and worthily magnify Thy Holy Name." These prayers I have long ago committed to memory, and find more helpful in many life situations that to coin my own verbiage in talking with my Father who art in heaven.

Search the Scriptures

"All scripture is inspired… for training in righteousness" (I Timothy 3:16). The sense of the term "means of grace" is certainly implied in this text. The great sin of omission for most Christians is evidenced by our biblical illiteracy. The reason we so easily fall prey to false doctrines is that people manipulate the Scriptures and play biblical hopscotch. We have not mastered the Bible enough to counter those who confuse us. In essence, Wesley advised us to take the "micro" texts and project them onto the "macro" biblical message. If they do not seem to fit, determine if the text "computes" with the larger message and mission of Jesus.

Article of Religion #V reads, "The Holy Scriptures containeth all things necessary for salvation." (The insistence on "plenary inspiration" of the Bible was never a phrase until 1918). With all the good benefits of biblical criticism since the mid-19th century, scholars have often dissected the Bible and never put it together again! That is like a surgeon who would remove our organs for examining, then not put us together again! We must search the Scriptures for language, cultural context, theological context, and style of literature, but we must never lose sight of Scripture as the Word of God, holistically and redemptively.

Charles Wesley is our best teacher here:

> Whether the Word be preached or read,
> no saving benefit I gain
> from empty sounds or letters dead;
> unprofitable all and vain,
> unless by faith thy word I hear
> and see its heavenly character.
> If God enlighten through his Word,
> I shall my kind Enlightener bless;
> but void and naked of my Lord,
> what are all verbal promises?
> Nothing to me, till faith divine,
> inspire, inspeak, and make them mine.[12]

Searching the Scripture is different from Bible study or sermon preparation. We are not "strip mining"; we are "deep drilling." We need first to do our study, learning all we can from commentators. Then to "search the Scripture," we must have only the Bible and a place of meditation and focus. Read it slowly, sometimes word by word. Stop and meditate on its meaning. Flora Woellner compares this to soaking in a tub of warm water, letting our body absorb the calming, cleansing effects of the water. As an example, take a moment just to soak in the truth of Psalm 36:7, 9: "How precious is your steadfast love, O God, all people may take refuge in the shadow of your wings… for with you is the fountain of life; in your light we see light." Charles Wesley prays in a song, "Unlock the truth, thyself the key, unseal the sacred book."

The Lord's Supper

Of all the strengths of frontier Methodism, its revivalistic legacy, and its circuit-system polity, the greatest loss was the spiritual grace associated with the sacrament of the Lord's Supper. Only the African-American children of Wesley kept the sanctity and theology of Wesley regarding Holy Communion. Wesley insisted: "1) That the Lord's Supper was ordained by God to be a means of conveying to men either preventing or sanctifying grace, according to their several necessities. 2) That the persons for whom it was ordained are those who know and feel they want the grace of God either to restrain them from sin or to show their sins forgiven." 3) That there is no previous preparation necessary but a desire to receive whatsoever he pleases to give. And 4) that no fitness is required at the time of communing but a sense of our state or need.

One Methodist fundamental regarding Communion is that we invite people to Jesus' table, not to a "Methodist" table. Therefore we have "open communion" with no regard for church membership.

We will never know the full meaning of baptism and the Lord's Supper on this side of heaven, but in recent years, considerable consensus has developed around two terms: "holy mystery" and "real presence." The Eucharist is indeed a means of grace we neglect to our spiritual peril.

Holy Conversation

Wesley's diary is sprinkled with almost daily references to time spent during his Georgia missionary pastorate in "necessary talk" or "holy conversation." In recent times this term has been morphed into "holy conferencing." One is reminded of the adage that "great minds talk about ideas, mediocre minds talk about events, and small minds talk about people." My mother often told me, "You are known by the company you keep." Though she meant my reputation — and the likelihood of being influenced by bad habits, such as smoking and drinking and using profanity — at a much deeper level, her advice is still more correct. If we hang out with sports fans, our conversation will almost by necessity require lots of homework in statistics of athletics and their teams. If we hang out with persons of a committed political ideology, we shall most like encourage each other to hate the opposite political party and all its leadership. And if we hang out with drug addicts, it will be difficult for us not to eventually indulge. However, if we hang out with people who are reading, thinking, praying, doing justice, loving mercy, and walking humbly with God, we will likely adopt that lifestyle and discipline as our own.

Carlyle Marney, founder of a clergy retreat center called "Interpreters' House," wrote a significant book called *Priests to Each Other*. I transposed that years ago into "priest at your elbow." The message convinced me years ago that every Christian needs "a priest." This means someone who is a bona fide soulmate with whom one can exchange the journey of souls, the peaks and valleys, the doubts and fears, the joys and God-moments. Marney insisted that this should not be your spouse but someone more physically detached. Also it is a myth that any one person can meet all the needs of another person. He urged pastors not to choose another pastor of the same denomination. We always run the risk of betrayal, and denominational colleagues are more apt to yield to that temptation!

The point is that "the heart is a lonely hunter," and we need to find someone who is indeed like the priest in the confessional booth of Catholic tradition, not as an intermediary with God but as a confidant. If holy conversation is the essence of these relationships, it is not either of us becoming more like the other, but both becoming more like Jesus.

Leonard Sweet has recently written an important book called simply *11*. He takes eleven biblical characters, gives them a psychological/theologically descriptive title, and advises that each of us needs the counterpart of a Nathan the prophet who will tell us what we need to know about our sins, a Jonathan who will be a true friend, a Barnabas who will be the "encourager," a "little one" like Rhoda, some "VIP's" like Lydia and Lazarus, and a sacred place like "Jerusalem."[13]

Sweet always sprinkles his books with pregnant quotes, one of which in this book is from psychologist and author Larry Crabb: "The Church is a community of people on a journey to God."[14] Sweet cites Mark's word about Jesus: "Jesus appointed Twelve… that they might be with him." If Jesus needed twelve, why do we Christians think we can go it alone? I often hear from clergy the sad words, "I have many acquaintances and no real friends."[15]

The entire cultural history of the West has made us loners. Almost every facet of our life discourages trust and soul-sharing. Even in marriage, so many couples realize when the children are grown that the two adults who once married each other no longer know each other! We not only need a friend in Jesus; we need Jesus friends. Another profound insight of William Young in *The Shack* is Mack's asking Papa, Jesus, and Sarayu (who are his depiction of the Trinity), "Who's in charge? Don't you have a chain of command?" Jesus answers, "Chain of command? That sounds ghastly." Sarayu (the Holy Spirit) comments, "We are in a circle of relationship, not a chain of command. Humans are so lost and damaged that to you it is almost incomprehensible that people could work together or live together without someone being in charge. This is why experiencing true relationship [with God] is so difficult."[16]

At another point, Papa tells Mack, "It is all about love and relationship. All love and relationship is possible for you only because it already exists within Me, within God myself. Love is not the limitation; love is like the bird's flying. I am love." (As if on cue, the little bird in the windowsill flew up, up, and away!)[17]

Sweet describes God's "dream team" as the "Triple F's"—Faithful Friends Forever. I think Wesley was onto something that might be even more necessary in the 21st century than it was in the 18th. Until the 1850s, the essential socio-spiritual vehicle for Methodists was the class meeting; the Sunday school system unintentionally replaced it. Today we need to re-invent some version of the class meeting. We need holy conversation!

Fasting

Wesley fasted. Every Wednesday and Friday, he ate nothing until the afternoon traditional English "tea time." He saw food as fuel to provide him energy for his work, not as an indulgence to be enjoyed for its own sake. He never encouraged fasting to the point of harming one's health, but did see it as a spiritual discipline; indeed, as a means of grace. For the most part, Methodism has neither taught nor practiced fasting as a means of grace. With the increasingly serious problem of obesity in Europe and North America, we need to look anew at the stewardship of the body. Fasting undoubtedly is needed to cleanse the body of toxins. Our diet has far too many food additives, sugar substitutes, and trans fats. If we do not see fasting per se as a means of grace, we certainly need to see temperance at the table as a means of health — physical, emotional, and spiritual.

Public Worship

In Wesley's lifetime, he never acknowledged Methodism as a church;

to him it was a movement of renewal within the Church of England. He never allowed Methodist societies to meet at "church hours." He insisted that a means of grace was the Sunday worship service of the parish church. By the 20th century, Sunday morning worship had become the major paradigm for "building up the saints" in all denominations.

The church belongs in this list as a "means of grace." The church is God's mission to the world; it is not an end in itself. The sad mistake of the 20th century was to develop a sophisticated "church-ianity" that was not synonymous with "Christ-ianity." We developed "churchmanship" (male and female) rather than discipleship. We assimilated new members by placing them on finance committees and program teams when they were babes in Christ looking for soul nourishment.

Worship within the church lifts us beyond the church to God. Gothic architecture did that in the Middle Ages, but now we must use other means. Music is a marvelous vehicle — both instrumental and vocal. So is preaching. Few exchanges in one's life surpasses an honest preacher sharing with a congregation what he or she has experienced with God.

EPILOGUE

This little volume is dynamically indicative, not limitingly definitive and certainly not exhaustive. Perhaps the best format would have been to leave blank pages for you to write your own additional chapter of what is "fundamental" for you.

Too little has been said here about social justice. That is a dimension of perfecting grace that needs its own treatment in another volume.

My fondest hope is to hear that Sunday school classes, small groups of diverse names and settings, individual laity, and clergy will find these pages helpful. As the current pastor of a church that is not United Methodist, I can see usage far beyond the writer's confines of Methodism. Every Christian needs to "work out your own salvation in fear and trembling for it is God who is working in you, enabling you both to will and to work for his good pleasure" (Philippians 2:12).

"It is hard to find words in the language of men to explain the deep things of God. Indeed there are none that will adequately express what the Spirit of God works in his children. But perhaps one might say by 'testimony of the Spirit' I mean an inward impression of the soul, whereby the Spirit of God immediately and directly witnesses to my spirit that I am a child of God, that 'Jesus Christ hath loved me and given himself for me'; that all my sins are blotted out, and I, even I, am reconciled to God."

Sermon: "Witness of the Spirit, I"

"What is the faith through which we are saved? It is in general a faith in Christ — Christ and God through Christ.... it is not barely a speculative, rational thing, a cold, lifeless assent, a train of ideas in the head, but also a disposition of the heart."

Sermon: "Salvation by Faith"

ENDNOTES

Introduction
[1] Halford Luccock, et. al., *The Story of Methodism*, Abingdon, 1926, 58

[2] An e-mail Bishop Carder sent to the author on Jan. 5, 2010.

[3] Gilbert Rowe, *The Meaning of Methodism*, Cokesbury, 1926, 24

[4] Albert Outler, ed., *The Works of John Wesley*, Abingdon, 1986, Vol. III, "On Laying the Foundation of The New Chapel" 585

[5] Edwin Mouzon, *Fundamentals of Methodism*, Methodist Publishing House, South, 1924, 16

[6] Ibid. 36

[7] Edwin Lewis, *The Faith We Declare*, Cokesbury, 1939, 48

[8] Ibid. 91

[9] Rowe, 151

[10] Lewis, 117

[11] Robert Cushman, *Experimental Divinity*, Kingswood, 1989, 100

[12] Ibid. 188

[13] Ibid. 189

[14] Ted Campbell, *Methodist Doctrine,* Abingdon, 1999, 19

[15] Ibid. 20

[16] Cushman, 21

[17] Outler, Vol. II, "Catholic Spirit" 93

[18] Outler, Vol. I, "The Way to the Kingdom" 220-221

[19] Ibid. 231

[20] Cushman, 186

[21] Randy Maddox, *Responsible Grace*, Kingswood, 1998, 150

[22] William Abraham, *Waking from Doctrinal Amnesia*, Abingdon, 1995, 59

Chapter 1: Methodism begins with John Wesley
[1] The term "rise" was first used by Wesley, then by Bishop Holland McTyeire in his 1886 volume, but lay dormant in Methodist nomenclature until restored in 1995 by Richard Heitzenrater in *Wesley and the People called Methodist*.

[2] Luccock, Hutchinson, and Goodloe, *The Story of Methodism,* Abingdon, 1926, 58

[3] Methodist historian Richard Heitzenrater corrects those who define Wesley's "social holiness" as 20th century "social justice." He notes that Wesley was a political conservative who believed in"acts of kindness and mercy and grace." Wesley was not a Liberation Theologian!

[4] William E. Sangster, *Methodism Can Be Born Again,* Epworth, 1938 (book title)

Chapter 2: Fundamental # 1
Methodists are Arminians – What is That?
[1] William Paul Young, *The Shack*, Windblown Press, 2007, 187
[2] Richard Heitzenrater, *Wesley and the People Called Methodists* Abingdon, 1995, 268
[3] Rick Warren, *The Purpose Driven Life*, Zondervan, 2002, 22-26
[4] Young, 185

Chapter 3: Fundamental # 2
"Way of Salvation" Begins With God's Character – Love
[1] Young, 102
[2] Jerry Walls and Joseph Dongell, *Why I Am Not A Calvinist*, IVP, 2004, 220
[3] Maddox, *Rethinking Wesley's Theology*, Kingswood, 1998, 39
[4] Outler, Vol. III, 542
[5] Outler, Vol. III, "Free Grace" 547
[6] Ibid. 555
[7] Outler, Vol. III, 556
[8] See Wesley's commentary on Romans 3:23 in his *Explanatory Notes Upon the New Testament*
[9] Rowe, 152
[10] *The United Methodist Hymnal*, United Methodist Publishing House, 1989, Hymn No. 387 Chas Wesley
[11] Outler, Vol. I, 578
[12] Ibid. Vol. I, 229 "The Way to the Kingdom"
[13] *The United Methodist Hymnal*, Hymn No. 339.
[14] Scott Jones, *United Methodist Doctrine: The Extreme Center*, Abingdon, 2002, 107
[15] Warren, 30
[16] Young, 191
[17] Young, 192

Chapter 4: Fundamental # 3
Preparing Grace – God's Love is a Seeking Love
[1] Lovett Weems, *John Wesley's Message Today* (Abingdon, 1982, 22
[2] George Matheson, 1982 (Hymn: "O Love That Will Not Let Me Go")
[3] Weems, 23
[4] Steve Harper, *John Wesley's Message For Today* (Zondervan, 1983, 39
[5] Weems, 23

[6] Rupert Davies, *Methodism*, Epworth Press, 1985, 85

[7] Outler, Vol. IV, 293 Sermon: "The Image of God"

[8] *The Book of Discipline*, United Methodist Publishing House, 2008, 46

[9] Walls, Dongell, 69

[10] Warren, *The Purpose of Christmas*, Howard Books, 2008, 22-23

[11] William Abraham, *Wesley for Armchair Theologians*, Westminster, 2005, 51

Chapter 5: Fundamental # 4
Sin is Real – The Evidence is Clear!

[1] Lewis, 111

[2] Outler, Vol. II, 170 Sermon: "Original Sin"

[3] Ibid. 172 Sermon "Original Sin"

[4] Ibid. 173 Sermon "Original Sin"

[5] Outler, *Evangelism and Theology in the Wesleyan Spirit*, Discipleship Resources, 1971, p. 29.

[6] Kenneth Carder, *Living Our Own Beliefs*, Discipleship Resources, 2003, 48-49

[7] Outler, Vol. II, 184 Sermon: "Original Sin"

[8] Ibid. 177

[9] Harper, 33-35

[10] Ibid. 32

[11] Outler, Vol. I, 143 Sermon: "Awake, Thou That Sleepest."

[12] Ibid. 226 Sermon: "The Way to the Kingdom"

[13] Ibid. 258 Sermon: "The Spirit of Bondage and Adoption"

[14] Young, 158

[15] Lewis, 197

[16] Jones, 153-154 and 221-240 (Chapter 8, "Social Justice As Sanctification")

Chapter 6: Fundamental # 5
Saving Grace – Co-operant and Resistible

[1] Outler, Vol. I, 187 Sermon: "Justification By Faith"

[2] Outler, Vol. II, 197 Sermon: "The New Birth"

[3] Ibid. 429 Sermon: "Marks of the New Birth"

Note: The reality is that almost every infant in Wesley's England was baptized at birth. Wesley's sermons, "Marks of the New Birth" in 1746 and "The New Birth" in 1760 cannot be synchronized with his father's "Treatise on Holy Baptism," which John Wesley published in 1758. Wesley never included baptism in what he defined as "the scriptural way of salvation," but he did include the new birth. He also did not include baptism as a "means of grace." Therefore, we cannot consider baptism a "fundamental." Wesley's doctrine of baptism remains debatable. We leave that to the scholars!

[4] Ibid. 199-202 Sermon: The New Birth"

[5] Abraham, 67

[6] Harper, 55

[7] Young, 126

[8] Harper, 55

[9] Outler, Vol. I, 405 Sermon: "The Circumcision of the Heart"

[10] Abraham, 66

Chapter 7: Fundamental # 6
We Can "Know Our Sins Forgiven"

[1] Rupert Davies, *Methodism*, Epworth, 1985, 51

[2] Outler, Vol. I, 285-286 Sermon: "The Witness of the Spirit II"

[3] Maddox, 168

[4] Outler, Vol. I, 287

[5] Davies, 50

[6] Outler, Vol. I, 298 Sermon: "Witness of the Spirit II"

[7] Abraham, 11

[8] Maddox, 84-87

Chapter 8: Fundamental # 7
Perfecting Grace – One Day at a Time, Dear Jesus

[1] Albert Schweitzer, *Out of My Life and Thought*, Johns Hopkins University Press, 1933, 59

[2] Colin Williams, *John Wesley's Theology Today*, Abingdon, 1960, 167

[3] Nolan B. Harmon, *Understanding the Methodist Church*, Abingdon, 1961, 70

[4] Williams, 175

[5] Harmon, 70

[6] Ibid. 71

[7] Reginald Ward & Richard Heitzenrater, *The Works of John Wesley*, Abingdon, 1990, Vol. 19, 97

[8] Cushman, 46

[9] Gerald Cragg, ed., *The Appeals to Men of Reason and Religion and Certain Related Open Letters*, Oxford, 1975, 163-165

[10] Outler, *Theology in the Wesleyan Spirit*, Discipleship Resources, 1975, 73

[11] Outler, Vol. III, 505 Sermon: "On God's Vineyard"

[12] Outler, *Evangelism and Theology in the Wesleyan Spirit*, Discipleship Resources, 2000, 125

[13] Harper, 93

[14] Carder, 63

[15] Hillary Hudson, *The Methodist Armor*, Publishing House of the Methodist

Episcopal Church, South, 1900, 110-111

[16] Outler, Vol. III, 74 Sermon: "On Perfection"

[17] Johnson Oatman, Jr.

[18] Carder, 63

[19] Walter Muelder, "Ethics and the Interior Life," *New Christian Advocate*, June 1957, 18-22

[20] Larry Goodpaster, *There's Power in the Connection*, Abingdon, 2008, 97

Chapter 9: Fundamental # 8
Mr. Wesley's "Means of Grace"

[1] Outler, Vol. II, 165 Sermon: "Scriptural Way of Salvation"

[2] Albert Outler, ed. *John Wesley*, Oxford Press, 1964, 357-358

[3] Outler, Vol. I, 396 Sermon: "The Means of Grace"

[4] Albert Outler, *Theology in the Wesleyan Spirit*, Discipleship Resources, 1975, 85-86

[5] Albert Outler, ed. *John Wesley*, Oxford Press, 1964, 347

[6] Abraham, 111

[7] Albert Outler, ed. *John Wesley*, Oxford Press, 1964, 356-357

[8] Outler, Vol. I, 376-377

[9] Thomas a Kempis, *The Imitation of Christ*, Revell, 1953, 47

[10] Outler, Vol. I, 380 Sermon: "The Means of Grace"

[11] John Greenleaf Whittier

[12] Charles Wesley, *United Methodist Hymnal*, United Methodist Publishing House, 1989, 595

[13] Leonard Sweet, *11: Indispensable Relationships You Can't Be Without*, David Cook, 2008, 14

[14] Ibid. 17

[15] Ibid. 17

[16] Young, 122

[17] Ibid. 101

ENDORSEMENTS FOR THIS BOOK

"Not long after I located to Salisbury, NC to assume leadership of Hood Theological Seminary, the Rev. Dr. Don Haynes, the author of this primer, was appointed as the senior pastor of the congregation of the First United Methodist Church in that city. From the time of his arrival in that position to the time of his retirement and unto the present day, Don has been a tremendous source of blessing to me in my ministry at Hood. One of Don's major blessings to me was his decision upon retirement, to serve this seminary as an adjunct instructor, in which capacity he has nurtured and continues to nurture many of our students and graduates through the tedious processes leading to the ordained ministry in the UMC.

Over these years Don and I have found in each other a strong passion for Methodism and the desire to share among Methodists and others the distinctiveness of our beliefs and the reason for our faith. Unlike other books that discuss the socio-political background in which Methodist took root and flourished in this country or the bases of Methodist beliefs, this primer describes in a compelling manner the fundamentals of our beliefs —what we do believe and why. As such then, it does not only inform us and others of our beliefs but indirectly invites them to become like us a "people with a warm heart." I highly commend Don for giving us such a timely primer of the fundamentals of Methodism and am convinced that its readers will find it a blessing."

Albert J. D. Aymer
President
Hood Theological Seminary

"Don Haynes writes out of deep commitment to Jesus the Christ and to the church in which he has served for his entire life, The United Methodist Church. This collection of essays provides a helpful view into the core beliefs and practices, and the uniqueness of this Wesleyan approach to living the way of Jesus. From a lifetime of experience as pastor and teacher, Don shapes these insightful and hopeful chapters at precisely the time we United Methodists seek to clarify our identity."

Bishop Larry M. Goodpaster
Western North Carolina Conference
The United Methodist Church

"This book will nourish your mind, nurture your soul, and inspire your heart. Read it to learn. Study it to enjoy both success and significance in life."

Nido Qubein
President
High Point University

"Any reader should profit spiritually from reading Donald Haynes' book On the Threshold of Grace. *The author grapples seriously with the contemporary meaning and application of basic Wesleyan concepts that have always been central to the tradition and without which one is hard pressed to claim a 'Methodist' heritage. The fast-moving text is filled with lively personal interpretations and illustrations that will draw the reader into a similar grappling with the Wesleyan view of the biblical gospel, which will certainly enliven and enrich their own Christian experience."*

Richard P. Heitzenrater
William Kellon Quick professor of church history and Wesley studies
The Divinity School, Duke University

"An engaging, lively, and faithful reaffirmation and fresh rendering of the marks, essentials or distinguishing beliefs of the people(s) called Methodist. An exercise in self-definition that goes back to John Wesley and has been updated time and time again by successive spokespersons. Laity will treasure and those on the ordination track will appreciate this readable essay on our evangelical doctrines."

Russell E. Richey
William R. Cannon Distinguished Professor of Church History
Candler School of Theology, Emory University